Table of Contents

3

4

Forsaking All Others and Holding On to One Another
Forevermore

A Final Word from Dr. Tina Scott

Foreword

Marriage is a wonderful phenomenon that can be intensely pleasurable as well as intensely painful. Pleasure is the result when marital partners operate according to God's original design for marriage. Pain is the result when one or both partners redefine God's plan according to their own definitions, desires, and circumstances.

God's plan for marriage occurs on three levels: physical, relational, and spiritual. Likewise, the pleasures and/or pains within our marriages will reflect in these ways. Such occurrences will take place on a biological level where two people actually become one flesh, on a relational or social level where two or more families are joined together, and on a spiritual level where two people serve as an ocular demonstration of the union of Christ and His Bride (The Church).

Marriage is not easy and even though the plan and prescription are outlined in the Bible, experiencing someone else's marital story is one of the best motivations there is. The testimonies found in *Wives on Fire* will not make your marriage pain free; however, the shared experiences in this book may lead to less pain and more pleasure in your marriage.

The principles you will gain from the testimonies found in *Wives on Fire* will help you navigate marriage's daily challenges and prove that God is faithful. The faithfulness of God is the testimony of Deidra Roussaw, who I have known for many years. She is a "wife on fire" with a passion for her own marital success and in this book you'll experience her passion to see the lives of wives transformed. Deidra's consistent coaching;

conferences and excursions (with numerous married couples) have inflamed the lives and marriages of many women at large. You will see this as you listen to some of the women she has inspired.

Wives on Fire contains simple everyday life choices that have led to pain and pleasure in marriage. You may have a mother, sister, niece, friend, or co-worker in need of this book – it's their opportunity to try marriage God's way.

Cleo Vilina Townsend, Ph.D., LMFT
Co-Pastor, The Resurrection Center, DE
Licensed Marriage and Family Therapist
Certified Anger Specialist

The Practice Marriage
Minister Deidra Roussaw

My boyfriend had been talking to my mom about getting engaged, and he informed me of his conversation and asked me to marry him. He was a good guy who was always applying himself and working to do better, so I agreed. He was highly intelligent, well-groomed and had a mind of his own. My family planned an amazing engagement party because this would be the first big wedding in our family. The only thing I had to do was show up! I was young and had no clue what a wife was supposed to do, but I went along with the plans. At the engagement party we discussed the wedding date, which would be the following summer of 1990.

In my heart I knew I wasn't ready to get married. I just thought we were too young. Getting married wasn't prevalent at that time, but I knew I would marry him eventually because he was a good guy. After having a family discussion, I knew everyone was excited for the upcoming wedding, except for me. I was trying to catch the excitement for myself; this was good news for my entire family after losing my dad. I just went with the program and wanted everyone to enjoy themselves.

The actual wedding PLANNING was a joy because I always loved organizing events no matter whether they were major or minor. I really just wanted to see my family happy. My brothers were remodeling my mother's kitchen, while we were off the do site inspections of the church and banquet facility. My mother invested a large amount of funds while making preparations, but I was already indecisive. I didn't have anyone to talk to about my feelings and I felt so alone. Something just wasn't right. My siblings were very supportive of their little sister physically and financially.

My fiancé had been "missing in action" on numerous occasions. I had concerns and suspicions, but the only person I could confide in was my girlfriend at work. Deirdre was a sister-friend who I confided my inner thoughts to and was always willing to assist.

A few days before the wedding my fiancée picked me up in a car he rented for our wedding, and we were heading to the church for rehearsal. After entering the car I noticed he was wearing a new outfit, sneakers and cologne. I began steaming because my mom had just put out a bunch of money for our wedding, and we were supposed to be making sacrifices in order to assist. I couldn't believe he was out making purchases to impress someone else. He rarely, if ever wore cologne so that was a red flag. While driving to the rehearsal we both stated we weren't ready to be married, although we were in agreement we would have to explain this to our families and the priest.

Upon entering the church, we met with the priest to explain our emotions. Everyone was on pins and needles wondering what we needed to speak with the priest about. The priest departed the Rectory and returned to the church without us to announce there would be no wedding. The atmosphere turned hostile and everyone was in an uproar, especially my siblings because my family had invested so much money into the wedding. My sisters were crying while I was trying to figure out why they were so emotional. I started crying because I felt the hurt of so many people by having second thoughts. My brothers were aggressive because they weren't aware of the situation; they were concerned for their little sister. Thankfully, my mom was at home making preparations for the reception, so that made it a bit easier. My entire family worked diligently and was very disappointed.

My fiancée grabbed me to take a walk, and he pleaded for us to go through with the wedding. After seeing the faces of the ones I loved the most I agreed! When I returned home my mother was awaiting my arrival, she inquired about what transpired. I explained, while crying, that I didn't know what was wrong but that something just didn't seem right. My intuition told me my fiancée was cheating, but I couldn't share that information with anyone nor did I know how. My eyes were so weak from crying; I wanted to be left alone, but my daughter held me while whispering she loved me. This instantly made me feel better and I knew I had to get myself together.

The wedding day was here and I was in shambles. I just wasn't prepared to marry this man whom my entire family adored. I was about to perpetrate for my family and so was he. He wasn't ready to get married either but his reasoning was very different. I couldn't wait to get this charade over; only if my dad was still living he would have given me some insight. I was really missing my dad; I was always able to confide in him about anything. The first man whom I loved dearly was the void that I needed so much to be filled.

After the festivities ended, my new husband was ready to leave, and I informed him I wasn't departing with him. On his way out he mentioned to my sister Flo that I didn't want to leave with him. My sister came into my bedroom pleading and crying for me to go with him. I finally decided to exit with him, but I knew in my heart he wasn't honest and something would later cause me great pain.

On that very day we separated! The only person I could share this with was my girlfriend Deirdre. My family thought I went on a honeymoon with my new husband, but I stayed over my other girlfriend Roxanne's house for a few days trying to figure what I had gotten myself into, and what would be the outcome.

Once I returned home I received plenty of messages from people who were trying to contact me. One person called three times, which was strange because this was one of my husband's friends who was supposed to have been in the wedding. I returned his call only to receive some heartbreaking news. When I inquired about him dropping out of the wedding at the last minute, he remained silent.

He then informed me that my husband was having an affair with a woman who worked at the hospital with them, and that she had been a guest at my wedding. The deceitfulness had made him opt out of the wedding. At that very moment all I could think about was the heaviness I felt leading up to the wedding. I immediately called my husband to obtain validation, and he asked me to meet him at the park later that day to discuss the situation. We met a few hours later and he confirmed everything. Words could not explain my emotional state, and he cried continuously and apologized. He pleaded for me not to expose him, and I agreed because exposing him would make me look insane. He contacted his mistress to inform her that I knew of her and he wouldn't be seeing her again. At that point my love started dissolving for this man. This was a man who pursued me continuously, yet spent money he really didn't have to impress the chick on the side while my family funded the majority of the wedding. He drove around with her the entire weekend in a car he rented for our wedding, and not to mention he'd invited his mistress to our actual wedding. I couldn't wait to see my wedding pictures and the video of this woman who would have the audacity to attend my wedding. I was aggressive and ready to create a situation with his mistress woman to woman!

The Death of my Brother

Two weeks after the wedding I received a call from someone in the neighborhood stating my brother Michael had been shot, and he thought my brother was dead because the guy who shot him emptied all the bullets in him. After informing my family we all jumped up and started gathering our belongings to proceed to the hospital. When we arrived at the hospital we were informed he was transported to another hospital with a trauma unit. When we arrived at the other hospital, my brother was gone. They allowed us to see him and we lost our composure as a unit. Our sibling circle was broken! My brothers Darryl, Russell, Gary (now deceased), Reggie and Bobby were our strength in the time of mourning! My brothers were always our rock!

The person I could always depend on and seek advice from was now a memory. My eyes were so puffy from crying and my nights were sleepless. I felt so awful for my mom. She was always such a good mother and now her heart was shattered. She had lost her baby boy. The last person to see my brother was my daughter since he took her to summer camp that morning. We never got the chance to say "Good Bye."

I knew that very moment things would never be the same. First my dad, and then my brother. I questioned God on all levels. I couldn't understand why he would take two of the most important men in my life away within nearly 16 months apart. I had no one to talk to who could understand my pain. My entire family was filled with grief that we had never felt before; I didn't know how we could make it. We were all clueless.

My Aunt Jackie, Aunt Margie and Aunt Anna (who have now gone home to be with the Lord) were at our house daily assisting my mom with the arrangements for the services. My Aunt Doris was an older cousin who always had a kind word;

she's such a jewel to our family. These women had so much love for the family and they kept my spirits lifted. They were HEAVEN sent. They knew exactly what to say and do; I so needed them at that moment.

They day of the service we were all loaded into the limousines ready to proceed to the church for my brother's home going service. My family arranged for my husband to ride in the limo with me and my sisters Flo, Pam, Pearl & Nicole. My mother thought he would be able to console me. We waited for him as he strolled down the street slowly without a care, and I immediately thought to myself that I never got the chance to tell my brother that the husband he encouraged me to marry turned out to be a cheater.

After the repast everyone proceeded to leave, and I would be lonely as I had a great fear of death. I really didn't understand death but I knew my father and brother were together again and looking over my family. I was sleep deprived; I had a fear of going to sleep. I was maintaining in the day but when the night fell something in me wasn't right. I started sleeping in the room with my sister and I think she was afraid as well. I read the entire Bible (King James Version) within a few weeks but I still could not shake this fear of death, nor did I understand what I was reading. I couldn't get a clear vision on why I lost my dad and brother. I only wished that I had someone who had solid and personal relationship with God to guide me.

Leading up to the wedding and prior to my brother's death, I was laid off from the Post Office. I had an abundance of time on my hands. My daughter was now five and about to start Kindergarten. My Uncle Arthur had become ill and was relocated to our house. My mom would begin the journey of caring for her brother, she was known to nurture and provide a safe haven for all of us. She was feisty yet compassionate!

My life had become a downward spiral, I was unsure of my destiny. The death of my dad, the death of my brother, and the separation from my husband had withdrawn so much of my energy. I was glad I had been laid off because I needed time for my thoughts. Being separated had begun to make my husband bitter; he was so mean spirited and cold towards me. I tried to stay away from him, and I thought who is this man was that he'd become. He started reaching out to be reunited with me, but I was afraid to be hurt again and I didn't deem him to be trustworthy. One day he stated he wanted to have a serious conversation between a husband and wife. I agreed to meet him over at his house. I arrived prior to him and did a bit of snooping in his room. If we were going to work on our marriage I needed to be sure I wouldn't get hurt again. I found a few telephone numbers which were prior to our relationship, which were altered. I thought I'd hold onto the numbers just in case I needed them at a later date. When he arrived he stated how much he loved me, how miserable he was without me, and asked if I'd receive his apology. Well, this man was so prideful and arrogant that I didn't want to make a hasty decision. I informed him that I needed time to process all that was stated. I couldn't figure out why all of a sudden he'd wanted to work on the marriage after all the hurt, pain, and agony he caused. Was it because people knew we were newly married and he was embarrassed of not being seen with me, or was it genuine?

A few days later my uncle passed away. I was so depressed because we were faced with yet another death in the family. I was at my breaking point and couldn't understand why all this was happening around the same time. My sister Pearl invited me to her house for breakfast, and my daughter started Kindergarten that very day so I decided I'd take my sister up on her offer. I agreed to spend the day with her until it was time to pick my daughter up from school. Prior to me leaving home I received a telephone call from the photographer stating my video and proofs from the wedding were ready for pick-up. Since I was eager to see my husband's mistress, I made my way to the studio. When I arrived to my sister's house, she was excited to see the video and the pictures. After seeing the pictures I knew exactly who the mistress was, this woman was dancing and having a good time as if she wasn't the mistress. I started thinking about the entire conversation with my husband about reconnecting; this would be an intense struggle for me, I was feeling very unsure.

I still had the telephone numbers in my wallet that I retrieved from his house. I thought I'd see if there were any involvements with the women of the numbers. Two of the numbers weren't legible because they were too old, but I was able to figure out one number. When I called the number a gentleman answered the phone. When I asked for the woman he inquired about who I was, and I stated I knew her from school and was trying to reconnect with her. He stated she lived with his grandparents and gave me the number. I wondered, "Who just gives information up so easily?" However, I proceeded to call the number. Her grandmother answered stating she wasn't home but volunteered information on when she would be in along with other information, I was amazed on the amount of information she disbursed. I called the number of the gentleman back to reveal who I really was. When the gentleman answered the telephone, I explained that I wasn't a friend of the woman who I later learned was his sister. I stated I found the number in my estranged husband's room and needed to know if they were involved, I informed him of the entire wedding situation including the mistress. He assured me that they weren't in any way involved and they were friends years ago from the neighborhood. He

16

stated he was supposed to attend the wedding and would like to see the pictures. He lived around the corner from my sister so I met him with the pictures. When he arrived I was shocked to see who it was. He knew exactly who I was on the phone but I hadn't known who he was.

This gentleman was so meek and humble; we sat on that corner for hours. He was just listening as I poured my heart out to him. I thought God had sent me an angel. I was able to talk about my father's death, my brother's death, my uncle's death, my wedding issues and the separation from my husband. It was such a relief; it was as if he was my confidant. This was so amazing to me and I was feeling good inside. I hadn't felt this way in months. I was so grateful and my peace was starting to be restored. He had to get ready for work and I had to pick my daughter up from her first day of school. He asked me to walk him to his house so he could retrieve his belongings for work, and I knew him so I wasn't skeptical. When we entered his home he went upstairs. I asked to use the phone so I could apologize to my sister for not returning to her home. He yelled for me to come upstairs, and I was shocked that he could have female company upstairs. I asked if he was sure and he responded, "Yes." When I entered his room it was like a love nest. His room was really neat, clean and he had lights around the perimeter of the room. I called my sister, she accepted my apology quickly and we ended the call. I turned quickly to depart his room, when he grabbed my hand and kissed me on the lips. It all happened so fast. I thought, "Why would this guy kiss me knowing I am married?" I felt like I had committed adultery and but I was separated. I knew that kiss wasn't supposed to have happened, so I dashed down the stairs to wait for him in the living room. When he came downstairs he asked why I had left his room so rapidly, and I stated that I wasn't comfortable being upstairs in his home, let alone his room, and I surely didn't appreciate him kissing me. He apologized and ensured me that it wouldn't happen again without my consent. We were able to do more talking on the way to the trolley and while riding the trolley. Before I got off at my stop he gave me his job number and stated if I needed to talk I could call him.

I was in such a good mood when I picked my daughter up. She was so excited to have completed a full day of kindergarten that she talked about her day the entire walk home. When I arrived home everyone had noticed a glow about me and they were inquiring about the transformation. For the first time in a long time I was able to come out of my shell and assist my mom who really needed me, since she had just lost her brother earlier that morning. Everyone thought it was because my husband, but to tell you the truth he was not a part of my new found joy. I just couldn't share it with anyone but my girlfriend, who was so happy for me since she was the one person I was able to confide in.

While thinking about the wonderful day I had, I decided to take the gentleman up on his offer and call him at work. I talked to him from 6:00 PM until 8:00 PM; the conversation was so good and genuine. I told him I had to prepare my daughter for bed and that I'd call back. After my daughter went to sleep I called him back at 8:45 PM and we talked until 11:00 PM. He called me when he got in from work around 11:40 PM and we talked until 5:00 AM. After I prepared my daughter for school, he called me at 9:30 AM and we talked until 1:00 PM. He had to get ready for work and I had to pick my daughter up from school. We followed this routine for the next few days and we were beginning to develop feelings for one another. He was off on Thursdays and Fridays. One Thursday, he came over for breakfast and it was good to have company that invested time in listening to my issues. One Friday after dropping my daughter off, he invited me to travel with him to Center City for some shopping and dinner at an elegant restaurant. My niece, Catina, volunteered to pick my daughter up from school and my other niece Fatima volunteered to babysit, so I would be able to hang out for a while. It was such a good feeling being out of the house and doing something different. This gentleman and I started doing so many things together. I started having a love affair with him; I would stay over at his house at times. I felt so safe in his arms throughout the night. This gentleman was so accurate and on point, and I thought, "Could this man really be so attentive to me?"

When I married my husband we were still living at home separately, which made things a lot easier with my new found love. This man was extraordinary; he used to have a crush on me in grade school. This love affair was incredible and indescribable. He would purchase me an outfit to wear to work whenever I stayed over at his house on weekdays. This man helped me overcome my fears. I was confused and torn. My family didn't know what transpired with my husband, and they eventually figured out that we were having problems. Since I was always gone they figured I was with my husband, but they never knew we were separated!

One day my husband called my sister Flo to inform her that we were separated and he hadn't spoken to me for days. He explained our entire situation to her, and she inquired when she saw me, but my love had dwindled for my husband. After my family had an intervention with me I decided to give my marriage a chance, and I told my friend I was going to work on my marriage. He was such a gentleman, and he agreed to step aside and allow me to focus on my marriage. I still wasn't trustful of my husband, so I applied for a job at the hospital so I could approach his mistress. I knew the affair had ended, but I just needed to have a conversation with her.

After I was hired at the hospital my husband and I bought a house, brand new cars, obtained credit cards together and even traveled a bit. When I got the job at the hospital my husband was worried because I was always a fighter and he knew I was eager to approach his mistress. When I finally saw her she was horrified because the buzz around the hospital was that I was looking for her. She was very frightened. She apologized and said she never meant to hurt me; as it was 2 years later. At that point I really didn't have any animosity towards her because I realized I wasn't in love with my husband any more. Since we worked in the hospital together we remained cordial. I knew this was growth for me because previously if someone hurt me I had to retaliate. It was in my nature!

At this point in the marriage I was Catholic and my husband was just beginning to study Islam. This was an additional strain on the marriage. I wanted more for my spirit, and I had so many questions about myself as a person and why was I put on this earth. How could I be married to one man but so attached to another man? Why did I fall out of love with my husband, and even more, why was I so unforgiving? Where did this unforgiving spirit come from and when was it developed? Why was I so bitter towards this man who I married? How did my love for this man convert from Eros to Agape love? I had all the questions yet none of the answers; I would later begin a quest to find the answers to my questions.

My friend Dwight and I were very clear on what we wanted but there were many obstacles. We continued to ask questions, such as if we were meant to be together why did I feel so bad or why does something so right seem so wrong? We didn't intend on hurting anyone but we couldn't seem to stay away from one another. We tried to do what was right, but little did we know that we were in warfare. We were in too deep, struggling with sin!

For we know that the Law is spiritual, but I am of flesh, sold into bondage to sin. For what I am doing, I do not understand; for I am not practicing what I would like to do, but I am doing the very thing I hate. But if I do the very thing I do not want to do, I agree with the Law, confessing that the Law is good. Romans 7:14 – 16

We both needed deliverance!

I had all the material possessions as a wife but I still wasn't complete. I remained friends with my Dwight's cousin Marty. We would visit various churches with our children on Sunday, dine out and maybe go to the movies or the mall. Our children loved dining out because it wasn't popular at that time. After visiting various churches I decided to visit a church that my family had always attended, so we went to Sharon Baptist Church. We continued to visit nearly a year before I decided to become a member. My husband's obsession with Islam had begun to weigh heavily on me because he was radical. I was learning the Bible, so we began to clash more often. I decided to seek employment at another hospital to gain my sense of self-worth. I was exhausted from arguing about religion at all times.

While in my new job I was offered a position to train a portion of the staff on a new system. One of the perks on this job was free or discounted tickets to theme parks, hotel discounts, rental cars, etc. Dwight's family inquired about purchasing discount tickets to an amusement park. I informed them that I would purchase the tickets for them. Dwight was the point of contact; he met me with the funds to make the purchase. He also had to meet me again to retrieve the tickets, and this opened up a whole new world for us. I was disconnected from my husband, so we began our love affair all over again. This time we took it to another level!

Then unexpectedly Dwight's brother was murdered, and Dwight felt so hurt, lonely and sad! I knew the feeling as my brother was murdered 4 years prior. I decided I would stand by Dwight's side, and as long as he needed me I would be there! This is a man of courage, who prior to his brother's funeral went to the funeral home to give his brother a final haircut. This act of kindness only made me love him more! My husband and I were not in agreement about me attending the funeral. When my brother was murdered, Dwight was a huge part of my healing process. The downward spiral would eventually ruin my marriage, which was already dying a slow death.

After the repast I was preparing to head home, and Dwight asked me to stay with him because he wanted me by his side. I felt that I was stuck between a rock and a hard place. I chose to stay because this gentle giant really needed me. One night turned into one week, which turned into one month, and so on. My family was very disgusted with me, especially my mom, as I wasn't raised to step outside of my marriage. The values were enforced more strongly on the girls than they were on the boys. As much as I loved my family, I was determined to be happy. This man made sure I had a smile on my face at all times.

We were so in touch and in tune with one another that we decided we would determine our own future. We decided to have an extraordinary relationship. We weren't trying to hurt anyone; we were in love and wanted to be together. Our thought processes were similar, and we wanted to create events that were memorable. We decided if we couldn't be together in our home town freely then we would visit various destinations. He had a large amount of family who lived in Maryland. Therefore, at least twice a month we would visit his relatives in that state.

We traveled to various destinations. We went to the Bahamas so often that we made friends with some of the natives and became God-parents to our one of the couple's son. They all traveled to the U.S. for vacation to spend time with us. This was an awesome feeling, being able to host Bahamians in the mid '90's in the US.

After all the island trips, cruises, upscale restaurants, shopping sprees, etc. I still felt empty, as if something was missing and I didn't know what it was. One day I heard a song, "Why We Sing," by Kirk Franklin, which started something in my spirit! When I joined Sharon Baptist Church, I went through nearly two years of counseling with my soon to be mentors Pastor Emanuel & Sister Martina Lambert. My pastor was factual; he meant business in our counseling sessions. Every time I went to counseling it was a battle because I wasn't used to the church jargon or clichés. On numerous occasions he already had the tissue ready for when I began to cry. This was a very painful process!

My husband and I separated more than a few times. I had outgrown him and wanted more. We created shenanigans which became embarrassing to both of us. The counseling sessions helped me define who God was calling me to be, and one of the things I learned from the 40 weeks of spiritual growth class was that my husband and I were unequally yoked!

Once I was very honest with my husband regarding my feelings for him and the love I had lost due to his infidelity, I was finally free. We started moving towards the divorce process which wasn't difficult at all, I appreciate my now ex-husband for being mature throughout the process. In the counseling process I learned that I needed to forgive him if I wanted to be free. I wanted the Lord to forgive me so I was commanded to forgive my husband. "For if you forgive others for their transgressions, your heavenly Father will also forgive you. "But if you do not forgive others, then your Father will not forgive your transgressions. Matthew 6:14 - 15

Dwight proposed to me during the divorce process and asked me to marry him. Of course I accepted because the man adored everything about me, and he wasn't perfect, but he was perfect for me. It was a journey but we managed to get through it.

He scheduled a counseling session with my pastor because he was upset about every time I had a counseling session I was an emotional wreck. My pastor fell in love with my now fiancée and began to counsel him separately. This was an amazing, feeling because we both were in counseling separately proceeding to live for the Lord.

When we told him we were engaged to be married, he was not in agreeance with it. He stated, "The divorce rate was exceptionally high for people who have cheated and decided to marry one another." My fiancée and I considered ourselves twins, and we were in sin together, but we knew we were in the deliverance process. My pastor and his loving wife worked diligently with my hubby and I. They even adopted my 9 year old daughter as their God-daughter; they were there for us every step of the way spiritually and financially. We were finally approved to attend premarital counseling and were one of the first couples where one of the spouses had been previously married.

We had a beautiful wedding; seven of our pastors and one of our ministers were on the program for our wedding. This wedding was what God had for us; we honeymooned in Bermuda, where we hung out every day with the parents of one of our pastors. We attended their church service on the island for the first time as Mr. & Mrs. Dwight Roussaw, and it felt good to be free in Christ!

One of the takeaways from my wedding was when my pastor, Bishop S. Todd Townsend stated, "It's you two against the world!" We literally took that to heart and started building a Christian marriage; we're always remembering that we were supposed to be a statistic included in the divorce rate.

A few years into our marriage we were invited to join the leadership team on the Marriage Enrichment Ministry at our church, and we took a few more years to decide. Once we agreed, we knew we had to excel, and the marriage ministry paid for my hubby & I to receive our certifications to become counselors. Over the years we hit a bump in the road and went through a winter season in our marriage. We decided to get other certifications which included teaching marriage classes. We were fortunate enough to have been one of the couples chosen for the late Dr. Myles Munroe's annual tropical leadership class which was held every April in Nassau, Bahamas.

We saw other couples struggling with the same things we were struggling with, so we did research to create an outreach marriage ministry. During our research we found that no one in the Delaware Valley had an outreach marriage ministry. Therefore, we were inundated with married couples, and the wives needed a little more so the Lord said create a marriage ministry. I didn't know what he wanted it to look like. At 3:45 every morning the Lord woke me up to give me instructions on what this ministry would look like, and he sent an awesome team of professional wives to help pull it off. As a direct result of my obedience to God, we were inspired to write a book called, "Wives on Fire."

Our pastors and mentors of more than 20 years, Bishop S. Todd & Pastor Cleo V. Townsend licensed my hubby & I on August 22, 2014 to become Ministers of the Marriage Ministry. This was the day before my birthday! How awesome is our God!

Within the last few months, the husbands saw the wives prospering within TrulyWed Wives. My husband heard from the Lord and started a husband's ministry called Husbands United. It's such an honor and privilege to work alongside my husband in ministry, and when we counsel, coach, and mentor couples, God gets the glory and our marriage grows due to our obedience to God.

My mom, the late Carrie M. Camp, passed away on December 17, 2014. This was the saddest day in my entire life. My matriarch and queen, who taught me so much, and gave me so much, was gone. She had kept me from harm's way. When I didn't know what to do or think, my husband, daughter, and grandchildren gave all that they had to keep me going. I was missing my mom terribly, our 6:00 AM morning chats were now a memory. I would weep for my mom alone; this was devastating for me. As I reflect on the way my husband covered me, it has made me love him even more.

As a direct result of being stretched in my faith, transforming from the mountain to the valley, I've become a radical for Christ. I know the feeling of being abased and abound. God promised that He'd never leave nor forsake me, Hebrews 13:5 b. I can only stand on the promises of God because in the time of trouble He shall hide me in His pavilion, Psalms 27:5. God has showed Himself to me during numerous times of adversity. I've learned to fear God only!

My life has been transformed into a wife such as Priscilla, who was the wife of Aquila. Priscilla served alongside her husband in ministry. When Aquila and Priscilla were mentioned in the scriptures, they were always together. Priscilla was serious about her faith in the Lord and her ministry. Her ultimate goal was to please the Lord by ministering to others about the love of Christ. This couple were lovers, friends, and inseparable.

"The churches in the province of Asia send you greetings. Aquila and Priscilla greet you warmly in the Lord, and so does the church that meets at their house." 1 Corinthians 16:19

I started serving in ministry with my husband in 2009 when we were researching information for our marriage ministry TWOgether Marriages. It's an amazing experience not only to serve in ministry with your spouse on the marriage battlefield, but serving married couples is a blessing which helps you build on your marriage while ministering. Learn more about the marriage journey in our upcoming book, Marriage on Fire.

Marriage is a good idea because it's God's idea,
The Late Dr. Myles Munroe

Minister Deidra is a wife to her loving husband, Dwight, mother of one daughter, Carrie, grandmother of 4 grandchildren (Kairi, Kayla, Kaleb & Kahle), wife coach, wife mentor, author, entrepreneur and minister. of Marriage Ministry at The Resurrection Center in Wilmington, DE. Deidra is the founder of TrulyWed Wives®, a wives' ministry offering wife coaching, wife mentoring, retreats & getaways, annual wives conference via Bringing Sexy Back to the Marriage (founder Gail Crowder), wives night out, savvy wife tool box - Prayer, finance, communication, infidelity, inspiration, blended family, healing, investments, marriage counseling, intimacy, couples' devotion, weight management assistance, image consultation, romance concierge, and date night.

Deidra serves as the romance coach offering pleasurable resources and romantic exposure for couples to partake in for the purpose of strengthening and enhancing their marriages. Deidra is committed to provide exuberant experiences that will invoke passion and devotion to the sanctity of marriage. She hosts a monthly wives-only prayer conference call, every Third Thursday which creates a safe environment for wives to pray, learn the word of God, and participate in a wives' dialogue. Deidra is co-founder of TWOgether Marriages® alongside her husband Dwight. They offer marriage coaching, marriage mentoring, they lead the Dynamic Marriage class, have an awesome "Date Night Program," and they host a one of a kind annual Marriage on Fire Retreat and Marriage Sailabration.

A wife of noble character is her husband's crown" ~Proverbs 12:4

To Have
And
To Hold

A Word From
Minister Precious D Graham

Before I could ever consider myself to be a Wife on Fire, I had to first ask the question, "What am I on fire for?" As I reflect on that question, I must first reflect on my relationship with God, and how the love I receive in that relationship correlates with the fire that burns in my heart for my husband. This is the fire that ignites my purpose on a daily basis. This is the flame that kindles my desire to hear Him, see Him, and feel Him in every situation I face. *This* is the consuming fire that wakes me up in the morning asking the Lord, "How can I serve you better today, while being the loving wife to my husband, and nurturing mother to my children, that you have called me to be?"

These are the questions that every married woman or even women that aspire to be married should ask themselves as they continue to grow and mature in Christ. Before we were married, we endured heartache and heartbreak, disappointments and discouragements, some of which were inflicted or introduced by our own hands. Some of us were single parents, working two or three jobs to make ends meet, and still recognized that our best efforts were not enough. Prayerfully; like the apostle Paul, we learned how to be content whether we had little or whether we had much. During our journey, we also learned that it was God who comforted our weary hearts and bottled up every tear along the way. Seeing God answer prayers, we forgot we prayed, how can we not worship a God who never forgets!

Yes, God has used the story of our lives, and the testimony of our faith, to mold and shape us into the women (and wives) we are today. In spite of everything we have gone through, we still hold on to the fact that we are fearfully and wonderfully made in God's image. That is why I believe "Wives on Fire" is a much needed resource for Christian wives for such a time as this. A wife on fire is one that fears the Lord, submits to her husband, and loves her children. She is passionate about her convictions and she carries herself with a spirit of excellence. She does not allow the world to define or limit her, and she is determined to break through every glass ceiling that hinders her growth. She understands that in spite of her faults and flaws, that she can still do all things through Christ that strengthens her. This is her witness, this is her story, and this is what makes her a wife on fire!

From Out of the Flames
Adrian McKenzie

There comes a time in every woman's life when she must take a closer look at herself. Who is this person glaring back at me in the mirror? She has many questions and is desperately in need of answers. Why is life full of challenges and adversity? What must I do to have a fulfilled life? She discovers the answer is quite simple, but getting there can be rather difficult. It would be like walking through a fire.

As a young child, both of my parents were in the home. Prior to their divorce, I saw and heard things that no child should ever bear witness to or experience. At the age of seven my father walked out on my mother, abandoning the marriage and his children. This experience left me confused, angry, and resentful for many years to come. As a result, I began to look for love and acceptance in all the wrong places. By the time I was twenty years old I found myself pregnant by a guy who cared more about the streets than me and his unborn child. Family and friends, much wiser than me, tried desperately to share their wisdom and guide me but I would not hear of it because I had all the answers. If I had only listened, I could have saved myself many tears. It was in this valley experience that I first noticed smoke. I told myself that I could not depend on anyone but myself to make things happen.

At the tender of age of twenty-three, I found myself skipping down the aisle with a man I barely knew. Two years later at the age twenty-five, I was pregnant with my second child. Like most marriages it started off exciting yet soon thereafter the love and respect was gone. Almost immediately, I began to recall images and memories from my childhood and I realized that many of the behaviors in my relationship were identical to my parents' marriage. I began to declare that no man would emotionally or verbally abuse or disrespect me in any way, shape, or form. After four years, I decided enough was enough—it was time to leave the marriage. With that choice I no longer had a husband and I lost all of my worldly possessions. This friction caused the spark that ignited a fire.

Life had thrown me a curve ball! This was my first taste of trials and tribulations and I knew I had disappointed God with many of my life choices. Every one of us will come face to face with adversity while on life's journey. It was during this season that I found strength and comfort in God's Word. God would bring scripture to my remembrance and drop bread crumbs in my mind and on my heart. I found myself meditating and chewing on Psalm 30:5 *"For his anger endureth but a moment; in his favour is life: weeping may endure for a night, but joy cometh in the morning" (KJV)*. Troubles don't last always and I knew if I could just hold on that God would turn it around for me.

Over the next year, I and my two girls were forced to live with my sister so that I could re-establish myself. Once again, I was alone, fulfilling the role of mother and father. I decided my top three priorities would be to devote my life first to my girls, secondly to work, and thirdly to the Lord. It was in these dark moments I realized the world did not revolve around me. As the blinders were slowly being removed, I learned that my life should not be centered on me, my daughters, or work but that it needed to be centered on the Lord. This one thought and declaration was the beginning of God's plan to turn my life around. You see, He had to first change my mindset. I

Thessalonians 2:4b tells us, *"We are not trying to please people but God, who tests our hearts" (NIV)*.

As I reflected on my life struggles, God revealed to me that many of my valley experiences occurred when I took my eyes off Him. It was when I got caught up on self, man, or earthly possessions that my world would come crashing down. It was in my dark and lonely moments I would cry out, "Help Me Lord, I Need You". I found comfort in Philippians 4:19 *"But my God shall supply all your needs according to his riches in glory by Christ Jesus" (KJV)*. Through prayer I would talk to God daily and I would ask for forgiveness and restoration. In my heart, I always knew He was there. Over time, God's voice became very clear to me because I included Him in everything and we developed a friendship. One day, I said, "Lord, why is it that every guy I have ever dated has cheated on me?" The Lord answered, "Because, you loved them more than you love Me." It was this conversation with the Lord that changed my life forever. I needed to change my attitude, make God the center of my life, and remain in constant communion with Him. I learned that I should never love anyone or anything more than my Lord and Savior.

After reflection, meditation, and prayer, I realized my priorities were out of order. With my new found truth, I decided to devote my life first to the Lord, secondly to my girls, and thirdly to work. This allowed me to study my past and acknowledge my mistakes and misguided motives. I released my anger, hurt, and disappointment and begin to work out a strategy for those things that were within my power to change. I became intentional on gaining control over my emotions and tongue. Through persistence and prayer, I learned to stand upright in adversity and not respond to every idle trick of the enemy.

All of my life, I have had faith. Faith as a child, that God would take care of me and my siblings after my parents' divorce. Faith as teenager, that God would provide food daily. Faith as a young adult, that God would provide for me and my children. For years, I would sacrifice myself for my children. I would deny myself small pleasures because there was always a bill to pay or an item needed for the children. My faith never wavered and through it all God sustained me and carried me through. God's word in Matthew 6:25- 27 tells us, *"Therefore I tell you, do not worry about your life, what you will eat or drink; or about your body, what you will wear. Is not life more than food and the body more than clothes? Look at the birds of the air; they do not sow or reap or store away in barns, and yet your heavenly Father feeds them. Are you not much more valuable than they? Can any one of you by worrying add a single hour to your life? (KJV)* Over the years, God has always been faithful and good to me! It did not matter if I was entering, going through, or coming out of a season, the Lord our God was always with me.

From out of the flames, at the age of thirty-five, I married the man of my dreams and my best friend. God knew I was ready because I was no longer looking to people or things to bring me joy and fulfillment. God showed His love for me by gifting me with a wonderful spouse and life partner. I show my love to and for God by loving and respecting my husband and being the best wife possible. I learned the hard way that my first love has to be God! This obedience to love the Lord first is why I and my marriage are greatly blessed.

Through worship, faith, and obedience, I discovered that God has set me apart and has blessed me beyond measure. In spite of everything I lost over the years God has restored it all tenfold. Despite not having any good role models for marriage and failing at my first marriage, God still saw fit to bless me with a good husband. I have a husband who is sold out for Christ and is by far the best husband and father under the sun. Not only did the Lord send someone to love me in all of my brokenness, He sent someone with enough love and acceptance to love my daughters as his own. In addition to having two beautiful girls, I gained two adorable sons to love and nurture. God said in Psalm 127:3-5 (KJV), *"Children are a gift of the Lord and a reward"*.

While in my valley, feeling alone and scared with a one-year old child, God blessed me with a job at a Fortune 500 Company. He opened up doors and opportunities that landed me a management position with only a high school diploma. I didn't know at the time that this was God's way of restoring me emotionally and giving me the confidence to push forward. Twenty-seven years later, in spite of numerous force reductions, I remain with the same employer. In 2010, after being out of school for twenty-five years, God nudged me to fulfill a lifelong desire to further my education. Four years later, I graduated Summa Cum Laude with a B.A. Degree in Communications and a B.A. Degree in Organizational Management. God took the brokenness from my early years to build my character and instill a passion to restore and encourage other women and couples.

Now, when I look in the mirror, there are no questions, just answers. I see my biblical ancestors smiling proudly back at me. Like Abigail, the wife of Nabal, I learned to look beyond whatever crisis may be going on in my life because; it's the tough situations in life that will bring out the best in you. Similar to Elizabeth, the wife of Zechariah, I learned that God does not forget those who have been faithful to Him. If I stare long enough, I see Priscilla, the wife of Aquila, in me. Priscilla and her husband were a power couple in the Bible who used their strength to complement one another. They were so inseparable;

they are never mentioned separately in the Bible. They opened their home and hearts to bless others.

Likewise, my beloved and I share a similar romance. In marriage and ministry, we operate as one. We use our home as a warm and safe place to train other couples on how to make the most of their relationships. Together we have an effective ministry that is dedicated to building marriages and restoring families. Through my trials and tribulations, I have learned to have faith, be obedient, and to put God first in my life. *"In everything you do, put God first, and He will direct you and crown your efforts with success."* Proverbs 3:6 (TLB). Let's not wait for trials and tribulations to remind us of where our priorities should be. The answer is simple; the Word of God says to, "Seek first the kingdom of God." Matthew 6:33 (ESV). Getting there doesn't have to be difficult because our God never gives up on us and desires to talk and walk with us every day.

Mrs. Adrian McKenzie is a Wife, Mother, and Co-Founder of Bread for the Journey Ministries. She is a Professional Mediator, Relationship Coach, Certified Marriage Instructor, and serves as Leader of the Covenant Keepers Marriage Ministry at the New Psalmist Baptist Church, Baltimore, MD. Adrian is devoted to building marriages, restoring families, and helping others experience the best in their relationships.

The Last Shall Be First
Dale Sharpe-Lee

The call to the ministry of being a helpmeet is not one that should be answered without spending specific time in prayer, actively pursuing a journey of spiritual maturity, and assertively making serious preparations for the leap of faith of when the two shall become one.

If you are like me, you may have had some feelings, thoughts, ideas, big hopes, and dreams of how wonderful life was going to be; married to the man of your dreams and being his wife. We, oftentimes; however, become lost and distracted by our thoughts and our desires. We fail to remember that our way is not God's way and our thoughts are not God's thoughts. Consequently, our internal journey directly impacts our external destination. As we give consideration to the idea of the last shall be first as it relates to marriage, it is important to consider that the value of first or last has more to do with internal posture than external position. In other words, where is your heart as it relates to your relationship with the Lord? The answer to this question will be the driver of your purpose and passion for your marriage relationship. The reality of the responsibility and ministry of marriage is not one for the faint of heart nor the spiritually, emotionally, physically, and financially ill prepared. We know that the Word talks about us not having because we have not asked. There are times when we don't receive what we ask for because we have asked for the wrong reasons and with the wrong intentions. Something else to be considered is that what we are asking for we are not prepared to receive. That old adage, "be careful of what you ask for", is a warning that must be heeded.

I have been married to my husband, Dr. Paul R. Lee, a Pastor, since 2006. This was not the first marriage for either one of us-which is why I chose to call my chapter, The Last Shall Be First.

In society there are a number of negative things said or thought about someone who is not the first wife so I want to remind anyone who may not be the first wife, to endure the challenge and have confidence that the Lord determines what is good. Hebrews 10:35-36 says, "Therefore, do not throw away your confidence, which has a great reward. For you have need of endurance, so that when you have done the will of God, you may receive what was promised."

When my husband and I got married I was 47 and he was 54, so clearly we were no spring chickens. We both owned homes, he had been preaching more than 30 years and I had been on my corporate job for more than 30 years. He had four children and I had three children and then we became the BLF (Blended Lee Family). There is no quick or easy process to developing a healthy and strong blended family. It is important to come to terms with the fact that you can't force feelings or situations. You have to diligently seek the Lord to allow Him to change you so that your entire blended family would have an opportunity to individually and collectively grow together. This growth process is not based on what you see on television or how someone else manages their household. You have to identify what works for your family and then work it. My motto is plan your work and work your plan. You have to be committed to demonstrating sincere Godly love for your entire blended family no matter how long or how difficult the task or the journey. Whether the love is given back or not, remember that Christ died for us while we were yet sinners, which means He didn't wait until we got it all together to show us sacrificial love. Therefore, we must trust the Lord's process and be patient with His timing. His process is not something you can go around. If you try to go around God I promise you will find yourself either in the same place where you started or much further behind. It is far better to spend your time and energy following the Master's plan and process.

There is no doubt that doing it God's way leads to tremendous work but it also leads to tremendous rewards and blessings (Deuteronomy 28:1-2).

As our story continues, neither my husband nor I was interested in having babies; we just wanted to participate in the festivities that come along with making babies. We told ourselves that as soon as we got married everything would fall into place; we would be able to have more time with each other, and our marriage and life together would be everything we thought was previously missing in other relationships. We were going to live the dream of the last shall be first. Well, the problem with unrealistic dreams is that they can quickly turn into nightmares. I came face to face with the many unexpected challenges of being married to someone who had been given an assignment by the Lord; an assignment that would take up 90% percent of his time. The unexpected challenges that I would gain a list of additional assignments as a result of his assignment; that I would face an intense level of scrutiny by people regarding what I said, didn't say, what I did, didn't do, what I would wear, didn't wear, where I sat in church or didn't sit, and the list goes on. Wait! That is not the entire story. I still had to work at a demanding, stressful corporate job; manage and take care of our home while responding to the needs of our biological and spiritual family; and ensure that I kept up with taking care of my husband's emotional and physical needs (which is a helpmeet's responsibility--sisters-like it or not we are responsible). Hold on, there is more. In the midst of what I thought was a demanding schedule, the Lord started to give me more work. Ok, now this story is about to come to an end so I thought. My cup was running over with this whole idea of the last shall be first. Based on what was going on I didn't want to be first, second, or third. Just count me out! I started to become overwhelmed, frustrated, tired, and disgruntled. I didn't like my husband, didn't like my life, didn't like myself, and at my lowest point, I wasn't too fond of the Lord either.

Clearly in my mind He was solely responsible for this mess because He let it all happen. At that point in my marriage the beauty of the two shall become one was starting to look more like two was one too many. During this time my emotions really were the driver of my behavior so my relationship with my husband was not one with which the Lord would be pleased.

It was very easy for me to blame my husband for everything that wasn't right with my life. I had a long list of why he was to blame: he was always busy, never took enough time out for us, never planned things for us to do or places for us to go, never did what I wanted him to do, and never handled things the way I wanted them handled. I was full of the never, never, never. I had brought a first class ticket to Neverland!

During this Neverland storm I cried many tears and often felt depressed, alone, and as if there was no hope of change anywhere in sight. I started reliving the old demons of the past that told me I wasn't good enough, I wasn't thin enough, pretty enough, light enough, smart enough, and the list goes on. Isn't it something how the things that you thought you were over and no longer mattered to you are the first things that come to your mind and heart when you are going through? This is why so often when we ask the Lord for deliverance He gives us development.

Only when we grow and develop are we able to be sustained through the rough times in life. Not only will we be able to be sustained, but we are able to grow through instead of grow up. You see, growing up happens as a result of time passing; but growing through happens as a result of passing through times. We can't get through until we grow through. During my experience of crying out my heart to the Lord I thought of how Hannah must have felt when she cried out to the Lord. Hannah was asking for the birth of a child and I was asking for the birth of a new me and the healing of my marriage. As a result of growing through, I had come to terms with the fact that I had to wait on the Lord (Psalm 27:14). I thank God that He didn't allow my Neverland experience to be the last and ending of my marriage story. The Lord helped me to hear Him speaking to my heart about my own stuff. He helped me to see that the very problem that I thought I was having with everything and everyone else was the problem He was having with me. I had allowed myself to be so engrossed in the what, when, where, how, and why of life that I forgot all about the Who that is in charge of all life. This is why we have to be so careful in life that we don't get trapped and sucked in by the busyness of focusing on the destination that we miss the joy of the journey.

I had to allow myself to have a posture of being last in order to position myself for the Lord to have an opportunity to move me to first. You see, I was able to say the last shall be first from my lips without any real understanding and conviction of the heart. At times it is such a long, hard journey from the lips to the heart, yet we must have faith to do the work that is required (James 1:3-4).

So I asked for forgiveness from the Lord and my husband (don't be too stubborn to ask for forgiveness). I had to let go of trying to be the author and the finisher of my faith and fate. I renewed my commitment to my prayer life and my individual and corporate study of the Word. I was determined to embrace the helpmeet assignment the Lord had given to me with a full appreciation of the assignment that the Lord had given to my husband; my protector, my provider, and the head of our household. This meant I had to take any concerns about time, needs, wants, and desires to the Lord and trust that the Lord would speak to my husband and create change when and how He determined it was needed (Psalm 37:7 and Psalm 40:1).

I also started to really think about who I was as a person. I had to be honest with myself, realizing there were things I didn't like about who I had or had not become. There were things I wanted to do in life that I blamed other people and/or circumstances as to why I didn't do them or couldn't do them. But the only person stopping me was me. So, I took off my breastplate of blame and put on my shield of responsibility and started the process of growing and developing into the image that the Lord would be pleased with. I am happy to report that BLF (Blended Lee Family) is doing well. We may not be perfect but we are perfect for each other. As for the Paul and Dale love story of the last shall be first let me just say in the words of Etta James song, "At last my love has come along and my lonely days are over". We are looking forward to, "The Best Is Yet To Come!"

Isaiah 40:31 "But those who hope in the LORD will renew their strength. They will soar on wings like eagles; they will run and not grow weary, they will walk and not be faint."

Dale has spent the last 37 years of her professional life in the financial industry at Wells Fargo Bank. For the past 20 years she has been using her talents, skills, and expertise as a Vice President in Human Resources specializing in Employee Relations.

More than 10 years ago she co-founded her first business with her Sister, Arlene Upchurch, called, "Save To Serve", a catering business. She is also the founder and owner of DFG (Destined For Greatness) Associates. She has been planning events and creating unique successful experiences for over 15 years. She has received numerous awards, recognition, and accolades for successful events and presentations." She is also the Executive Administrator of a women's organization called WOW (Women of Wellness) made up of 200 women from 54 churches located in 15 states.

Dale has occasionally utilized her organizational skills and talents working with the National Baptist Convention USA, Inc. through the Sunday School Publishing board as a Conference Administrator for their Christian Education Conference.

She is married to a wonderful man, Dr. Paul R. Lee, who is the Pastor- Teacher of Jones Memorial Baptist Church in Philadelphia, PA. The two of them have seven children and 11 grandchildren. She is grateful to be a breast cancer survivor since 2007. Her life's journey and desire is to continue to be a light of hope that we are all destined for greatness.

Finding Love Again
Dornell Watson-Dean

My name is Dornell Watson Dean, and I was born on June 8, 1965, on the beautiful island of Nassau in The Bahamas. My mother, Winifred, was 15 years old and raised me, her only child, as a single parent. I attended a public elementary school and transitioned to a private Catholic high school. My studies continued at The College of The Bahamas for 2½ years where I obtained an Associate's degree in accounting. Upon completion, I worked for three years in the Banking industry and saved over $15K so that I could attend college in the US. I left the Bahamas in January 1988 and relocated to Washington, DC, where I attended Howard University. I graduated in May 1990 with a Bachelor's of Business Administration in Hotel/Motel Management. I have been employed with the Bahamas Tourist Office for the last 25 years as a marketing manager. I am the mother of a beautiful, smart and intelligent eleven-year old daughter.

How I Met My Husband

I initially met my husband, Art, in the latter part of 1989. We met at a Bahamas Independence Reception in Washington, DC, through introductions by his older sister Dorothy, who was a very good friend of mine.

Art and I had a brief eight-month relationship. During our courtship, we discovered that we had a lot in common like the love of music including the same music artists, cooking, dining out, family gatherings, and fashion. Art was a true gentleman who would open doors and pull out chairs. He was also very romantic like holding my hand while out in public, planning candle light dinners, giving shoulder and foot massages, and giving me flowers just because he felt I deserved it.

Art was in a complex period of his life that led to the demise of our courtship. We went our separate ways for a period of twenty-two years. During that period, Art got married and had a son. I felt a tremendous void as I had never met anyone who wooed me, treated me like a lady, and romanced me in such a loving way. Nevertheless, I had to move on with my life.

Previous Marriage and How God Delivered Me to Move On

When I got married the first time in 1996, I got married for the wrong reasons. First, I was not completely over the man I considered to be my first true love while at the same time not in love with the man I was about to marry. Second, I was 31 and all my friends were getting married and I didn't want to be left behind and lastly, I wanted to have a big fancy wedding in the Bahamas with all the fanfare! There were also a number of red flags in the relationship prior to the marriage. My fiancé was not a Christian or a churchgoing man; he was a recovering cocaine and heroin addict, he had a dominating personality, and he was unemployed.

We initially met in Washington, DC where I was posted and then a year later I was transferred to Boston. We got engaged while I was in Boston and married a year later. The wedding and honeymoon in the Bahamas was beautiful! Then the real world set in. We came back and lived apart for 8 months. I was transferred to Philadelphia the following summer and my husband joined me. About three months later I realized my husband's behavior was very peculiar and discovered that he had relapsed! I sought help for him in a number of recovery facilities and methadone programs with no progress. For 3 years I had to deal with car seizures, arrests, court appearances, lies and deceit to get money, and a very sick man. I prayed constantly, attended Nar-Anon meetings, drove my husband to undesirable places to purchase un-prescribed methadone to help him feel better and stuck by his side until I could no longer physically, mentally and emotionally tolerate it any more. After all, I got married at 31 (my husband was 44 years old) and this was not my expectation of a happy marriage! I felt guilty for a while, but the reality was that I never left him when he was down and out. Instead, I endured the turbulence until he was able to take control of his life. Helpful Scriptures: Romans 5:3-5; Psalm 27:1-3; 2 Corinthians 4:16-18

Although I wanted to one day experience a blissful marriage, I was discouraged about finding love and giving marriage a second try. However, after ten years of being single and a single mom, I reconnected with the man, who made an impression on me more than two decades prior, the man I had dubbed the "Love of my Life"!

The Re-Connection

Art accessed my telephone number from his sister, Dorothy, and reconnected with me in 2012. At that time, I was residing in Pennsylvania and he was in Maryland. We dated for a little more than two years, reigniting the sparks that never died and getting reacquainted with each other and with each other's families. We had many stimulating conversations about love, faith, spirituality, aspirations, and family. We decided to take our relationship to another level...marriage! We then participated in counseling sessions and started planning our future.

Our Wedding

Given the fact that we'd both been previously married and spent thousands of dollars on lavish weddings in the past, we decided to keep our wedding small, intimate and inexpensive. We felt it was more important to focus on the marriage and not the wedding. Our ceremony took place at a Wedding Chapel and was officiated by my former pastor in PA. Following the ceremony, we had lunch in a private dining room of Houlihans with 25 of our closest friends and family members. It was a beautiful and memorable day!

<u>My Expectations of My Marriage</u>

I came into my second marriage with high expectations with the objective of having longevity, as we both felt failure or DIVORCE was not an option! I am determined to do my part to maintain a happy and healthy marriage. Once Art and I started living together, I quickly learned that this union called marriage was not going to be easy. If you want to know someone intimately, just live with him/her.

Marriage is not easy. It's a lot of work, requiring great communication, good listening skills, being quiet at times, being available to your husband when you're not in the mood, doing favors for your husbands when you don't feel like it, being unselfish, and simply compromising.

The following are attributes and practices that both my husband and I feel are important in maintaining a happy and healthy marriage:

- Be respectful to each other
- Say "I Love You" often
- Have the willingness to admit wrong and to apologize when wrong is done
- Have an active sexual relationship
- Worship together
- Pray together
- Prioritize each other and your marriage
- Never take each other for granted
- Compliment and encourage each other

- Make time to talk to each other
- Plan date nights
- Hug and kiss each other often
- Never say negative or mean things to each other because once said, you cannot take it back
- Be honest with each other and create a sense of trust
- Be creative and find ways to keep the spark ignited in your marriage

The Importance of Biblical Connection and My Favorite Wife from the Bible

After the honeymoon has worn off, reality kicks in. Things that started off fresh quickly turn stale. You begin to see imperfections and undesirable behavior and this is when we have to pray and ask God to make us like Him. We have to continuously pray for grace, mercy, humility, patience, and love for each other. These are the Scriptures that I have committed to incorporating in my married life: Psalm 51:10, 1 Peter 4:8, Ephesians 4:2-33, Mark 10:9, and 1 Corinthians 7:3-5.

My biggest struggle as a married woman is releasing my independence, as I was used to being single, paying my own bills, and making decisions without consulting anyone. I often have to remind myself that decisions are no longer self-made but made jointly. Another struggle is sometimes placing a higher priority on motherhood than my marriage, as my daughter is an only child. Despite these two struggles, I aspire to be a more faithful, God-fearing and respectful wife. The biblical wife who represented these qualities was Mary, wife of Joseph. Regardless of her circumstances, she listened to God and had a surrendered spirit to please Him. Mary submitted to the Lord in her difficult circumstances, which in turn helped her to respect and trust her husband.

Showing my husband respect and trusting his direction plus accepting his advice on many issues is a challenge for me, but a great one! As I work toward the goal of being like Mary, I will continue to pray, fast, and read supportive Scriptures like, Luke 1:38, 2 Samuel 21:8-11, 2 Kings 17:14, Deuteronomy 6:5, and Luke 17:5-6.

The Letter
Erica Bagwell

I recently had the privilege of attending a women's conference in Maryland. This conference is for women in all different walks of life who are ready to be changed and empowered by the Holy Spirit. I particularly was very excited because my big sisters in Christ had gone every year and this was my first time able to attend. I heard many life-changing things when they came back from the conference and I went with anticipation of what the Lord had in store for me. Because of my desire to be an effective leader, self-reflection is something I did constantly. While there were countless things that I walked away with the weekend of the conference the thing that was the most impactful to me was the assignment of writing yourself a letter as if you were 21. What would I say to myself at 21 with all that I'd experienced in the 15 years thereafter? What are the things that I would forewarn the twenty-one-year-old Erica if I knew what I know now? You certainly can challenge yourself to write that letter at another time. For the interest of this book and liberating and empowering wives, we will focus on writing a letter to your pre-married self.

Before I get started on my letter, I would like to tell you a little about myself. While my bio does a great job of giving you a visual of what I look like and tells you of my accomplishments and my wonderful family, it does not tell you who I really am. Who I really am is composed of all of those things and experiences in life that shaped me into me; and I can say they were not all glamorous as my bio would have you to believe.

There is so much more about me that even I do not fully comprehend. I have finally gotten to a place that I am okay with that. As long as I am still spending time with God, He will continue to uncover the layers that life and disappointment have hidden when the time is right.

So who am I? I am a lover of Jesus Christ and I acknowledge him as my Lord and Savior. All that I have and am able to do is only because of His grace and mercy. I am a wife of 6 years by the time this book is published. My husband and I have had our share of ups and downs, and those downs almost took us out. This is my second marriage and I pray this will truly be my "death do us part". He is my partner in life and a constant reminder of the power of forgiveness and second chances. While God is the source of my strength and joy, those three people that He made me mother of are my pride and joy. They truly keep me going and teach me how to love. I now consider myself as an overachiever because I spent so many years trying to figure out what I wanted to do and what I was good at that I stood in place and did nothing. At the age of 33, I decided to go back to school and get what I have been chasing for over a decade—a college degree.

I am the eldest sister of three children. Our mother unexpectedly passed away in 2012. She was our biggest supporter so life has been quite hard without her cheering us on. Yeah, I know, she is cheering us on from Heaven but sometimes, most of the times that is not good enough. One of last conversations she and I had was her encouraging me to go back to school and she is the reason why I strive so hard to do well in my classes. My passions are to help leaders serve in their full capacity and to see marriages represent how Christ loves the church. It was just this year that I realized what my life purpose is. My life purpose is to use my counseling skills to help people lose the shackles of the past, my life coaching skills to help people make the best choices for their future and my Christian skills to help people understand that you can't do either without Christ Jesus.

The purpose of our writing a letter to our pre-married self is for empowerment and strengthening. If you have been married for more than a day, you know this thing called marriage is work! In my counseling experience I know people tend to lean to the change him/change her approach but we must be aware that the most beneficial change is "Lord change me". Those 3 words represent so much power and strength. It acknowledges that I am imperfect, desiring to walk in my daily journey towards perfection. It accepts that there will be set backs and failures along the way. It confesses that it is not everybody else. It gives us confidence that "he who began a good work in you will carry it on to completion until the day of Christ Jesus" (Philippians 1:6, NIV). It gives us power to be a better us. Writing this letter is not an easy task, but if you take the journey along with me, I ensure there will be freedom by the time you close your letter. Remember, this is about you—your freedom, your breakthrough, your change. Get into your quiet space, grab a pen and paper or sit at your computer, make sure the box of tissues is near and let us begin our journey.

Dear Erica,

Before you enter into this covenant with this other person, you must be a whole person. This person does not complete you, only God can do that. He cannot be your father and be your husband; only God can fill those spaces. It is so important that you learn to love yourself first because expecting your husband to love someone you don't love is a huge expectation that you are putting him up against. Doing this will frustrate you and cause him to build walls what will be hard to break down. When you look at yourself in the mirror, you must believe in your own beauty so that on the days he forgets to tell you, you will still carry the same poise and confidence. He telling you that you are beautiful should only confirm what you already know.

Your beauty inside is more important. Yes, that smile may have been that thing that caused him to speak but it's that inner beauty that made him want to propose. You are more than wife-to-be. You are confidence, strength, graceful, intelligent and successful. There may have been some things that happened in life that may have striped you from that. If so, I dear you to wake up every morning, look at yourself in the mirror and say everything positive that you are until you believe it. You have to believe that it happened for a reason and God will use it for His glory and your gain. You are absolutely amazing and the gifts you have inside of you will truly bless others. In order to be it you have to believe it. So believe it! And more importantly, believe that God has put greatness in the inside of you; not to be used in competition with your husband, but to be used alongside of him.

Learn to forgive. Really forgive. Erica, the baggage that you are carrying into this marriage is way too heavy to bear. You have to let it go. You cannot make your husband pay for all the wrong things that other men have done to you. It is not fair to him and certainly not fair to your marriage. Un-forgiveness has torn so many lives apart and I don't want to see that happen to you. When you forgive, you allow yourself to be free from the person that hurt you. The first person that you must forgive is you.

Stop blaming yourself for how people treated you. No matter how needy you may have been, it was still their choice to cheat on you. Don't allow them to put that on you. Learn from it and move on. Stop comparing yourself to other women because there is only one unique you and there is something in you that made him choose you above all the rest. Trust his choice and stop looking for reasons why he shouldn't love you. He can love you and he does. You don't have to hide your imperfections because he loves those too and guess what, so does God.

There is so much I need to learn about myself. I hope can be great in my marriage. Even though I felt like my life and strength was depleted, the fact that I was able to function and be a parent to my daughter just amazes me. I truly found the meaning of God being my strength. I learned endurance and independence. What I saw in the mirror was not good but with each day, it begin to change and I liked who I saw. I still carry hurt and unhealed wounds but over time, those open sores begin to scab up, and leave a visible mark of healing.

As I begin the mental process of being someone's wife, I cast down every attempt the enemy tried to take me out of here. I acknowledge that it was the prayers of my family and friends that got me through. I know there were some that sat and watched to see if I would break but I didn't. God is giving me a chance to allow someone to love me with all of the mess that comes along with Erica. I am still scared, but I trust what God said to me even when I don't trust in myself.

I know there are indeed some things I need to do differently. I need to support my husband; and be his biggest cheerleader. That was something I failed at before. It is not all about me, it is about us. I have to support the vision my husband has for his family as long as it lines up with God's vision. When it does not line up, I have to be so spiritually grounded that I pray for God to intercede and get us back on track instead of shutting down like I am known to do. I have to understand the hurt that I had before, he did not do it! There will be things he will do but I cannot treat him like a defender on the witness stand for every hurt that I have experienced before him. I have to allow myself to heal so that marriage one will not roll into marriage two. I have to learn that he needs to be respected at all times. That is how he sees love and trust. Stop allowing that you heard about men to form how you treat him.

God, please teach me how to love. Not the love that I am comfortable with but the love in 1 Corinthians 13:4-7. I know it will not be easy because I've been doing it my way but Lord, I am submitting to you because only through you will I do it the right way. I know the previous experience was all for preparation so that I can help those that are going through the similar experience. Please help me to be transparent so that I can really help them through the aide of your Holy Spirit. Help me to love my husband as he needs but not put so emphasis on him that I leave You out. Help me to listen to him and pray that Your will be done in his life and not my will and what I want. Help me to remember that this marriage is not about me, it not about him, it is all about You.

Sincerely,

Myself

Wow, how liberating that felt! I pray this will give you the courage to begin your letter. If you are truly open and transparent, there will be healing that takes place. Once you are done writing, pray over it and allow God to minister to you. Rejoice that you were able to get through it and open the door for restoration. You will never be the same. Yes, there were some things that hurt and some things that we have to be accountable for but your latter days will be better because of it. If there were some areas that you realize you may need to get some help, then do so. You cannot effectively be a better wife if you are not a better person and you owe that to yourself. When you get the courage, share it with your husband. It will allow him to see a vulnerable side of you that he should grow and admire.

Thank you for allowing me to share that intimate part of me with you. If you would like to share your letters or your experience/breakthrough in writing it, please forward it to pearlswithpower@gmail.com. I would love to hear from you and encourage you through your transformation.

Erica's life verse is Jeremiah 29:11 "For I know the plans I have for you," declares the LORD, "plans to prosper you and not to harm you, plans to give you hope and a future" (NIV). This scripture reminds us that no matter what we may face in our lives, our hope in Jesus gives us a prosperous future.

Erica L. Bagwell became a Certified Christian Counselor in 2010 and graduated with her Diploma in Pastoral Studies from Palmers Theological Seminary in May 2014. She also became a Certified Life Coach at the beginning of 2015. Currently, Erica is attending Eastern University to obtain her Bachelor's degree in Organizational Leadership.

Erica was a featured author in *Moving From Struggle to Deliverance*, a collection of works to inspire women. Together with her husband Deryl C. Bagwell, Sr., Erica currently serves as a teacher and counselor to married couples.

Erica and Deryl have three children, Deryl Jr., Elantra and Essence.

God's Lead, God's Way
Jonise Stallings

When I married, my intention was to be married until death did us part. Well, after 30+ years we are still together. Yes, there have been some bumps along the way such as poor communication, disrespect, arguments and selfishness on either one or both of our parts. In the midst of all of this, there were some great times. Our greatest gifts were from God, our children and now our grandchildren. I think we forgot the order God intended. Instead of focusing more on our relationship and building a solid foundation, our children took precedence and we loved and sacrificed more for them than ourselves. We somehow forgot that a marriage is between the man and woman, and after God, it is the wife or husband who come next, then the children etc. Throughout the years we learned to intentionally lean on God; we gave Him control over our lives and because of His grace and mercy, we are still here together. The bumps we encountered were because of our pride and poor communication, which at sometimes challenged our trust and created a world of doubt about our love for each other.

As in any partnership, everyone must have an understanding of each other's wants and needs to establish a strong relationship. As I recall, when I became engaged not too many people that we loved and trusted shared any perspective about how to build a strong marriage relationship. I based my idea about marriage from what I heard or saw in my home, relatives, and other adults who were family friends or those images of strong marriages and families we saw on TV shows such as I

61

Love Lucy, The Cosby Show, The Jeffersons and so on. When I became engaged, my husband and I had marriage counseling but nothing that was detailed and consistent enough to teach us how to work through financial matters, parenting, accepting each other's differences, supporting one another, discussing our concerns or problems, forgiveness etc. We loved each other and for the moment that seemed to be enough. I grew up in church, yet I failed to allow God's Word to truly guide me in my marriage. In fact, the Bible says a man shall find a good wife. The question is did we women pursue the man instead of standing still until God confirmed the man for us? You see when we let God be the matchmaker a stronger bond will exist between the man and woman and the two can truly become one as God planned for marriage. I thank God for His mercy and grace. My husband did find a good wife, though not perfect, but faithful and devoted to my family and we are still with each other. In the beginning of our marriage, I accessed God when I needed Him. I wasn't consistent in leaning on Him during the good times or the challenging times. As I became wiser about our marriage and what I wanted it to be, I would often reflect on the story of the three pigs. I felt like the foundation of our marriage at times was like the pig whose house was made of wood. When obstacles came we were blown in different directions and could not come together to work through the issue. Instead, the problem faded away and we continued on until the next issue surfaced. We may have argued, let it go, and then it would fade away. We rarely took the time to discuss the issue so that we resolved it. What I really hoped for was a marriage that was strong enough to withstand anything that came our way, just like the third pig who built his house of brick, a house with a strong foundation, one that could withstand the enemy's (wolf's) effort to devour him, and it did. This house is the kind that only God can establish, if you trust, believe, and allow Him to do what He is able to do, which is more abundantly and exceedingly than anything that we could ever imagine.

The truth of matter is that none of us truly received a manuscript on how to have a strong and long-lasting marriage. We learned from our parents and others or we participated in some sort of marriage counseling. It was not until we lived together that we truly learned about each other's habits and behaviors. For me, some things were a real eye-opener and I am sure the same was true for my husband. We were raised differently and I noticed that both my husband and I tried to dominate and establish a marriage based on what we knew or gained from our past experiences. I guess you could say we were both selfish at times. No two marriages are alike. Couples must establish how they are going to co-exist in a loving manner to build a strong foundation for their future. There must be a give and take mentality as well as a positive meeting of the minds in order to create a wholesome and peaceful living environment. The other thing is that you can't change a person. I thought I could change my husband to be what I wanted him to be, and he repeatedly let me know that I had to accept him as he was. It took a few years, but I learned that the only person I could change was myself and turn it over to God, the only one who can change a person and break strong relationship barriers. I am thankful for the changes God has made in our lives. My mother once told me that they (men) get better with time. Just hang in there. I no longer tend to sweat the small stuff that use to have me arguing, stressing and wanting to leave the marriage. Comparing him to other men certainly didn't help. I learned to keep a healthy mind about things, so I continually pray for us and trust God to do the rest.

The truth of the matter is that you can't have a good marriage without God. I truly believe that in order to build a healthy and blessed marriage, and it's never too late to start, you must consider the following:

Allow God on Board, immediately! We serve a mighty God. He can do anything but fail. Make God a priority in your marriage and home. Husbands and wives must study the Word together, worship together and always lean on Him for help and guidance. Address the small issues before they become mountains. Always remember, when life throws you some curve balls, just pray and let God. Remember, His burdens are light and His yoke is easy. God said in His word, "if two or more should gather in my name, I will be there." What a comfort to know that He will be in the midst of your joy and challenges. All it takes is for you and your spouse to come together in His name.

Self-Reflection. This means searching your own hearts and motives. We have to leave the past behind and embrace new opportunities to strengthen the relationship. Take some time to look at yourself and habits before you commit to another person and if you are already committed work on making some positive changes to enhance your relationship with your spouse. Consider how you can be a good fit for the person you want to be or remain with the rest of your life. Remember, God gave you a glimpse of what you were going to get. You made the choice to be with your spouse and vice versa. Give your relationship your best effort and it will pay off. Don't be afraid to ask your spouse to help do his part. Women do a lot. Learn to ask for help. Don't assume your spouse knows what you want.

Friendship. Honesty goes a long way. Husbands and wives must open up and share past hidden agendas as they will eventually resurface and cause major issues for everyone.

Friendship is a necessity in any relationship. Learn to be friends. It will keep the joy, respect, honesty, etc. alive in your marriage or relationship. If you and your spouse are friends, you will know how to discuss and listen to each other's concerns and you will do so with the utmost respect. As friends, you will always have your spouse's back; you'll see the good in them and will pick your battles with the bad or smaller issues.

Love Yourself. Loving yourself will help you to build your own confidence and prevent you from getting stuck in certain roles for the man or yourself. Both of you must work hard in the marriage. Remember, you became one when you said "I Do." God said that men should love their wives as Jesus loved the church. Women are to submit to their husband, and remember you as the woman are a help meet for your husband. Just think, if both men and women would only do what God has ask of them, divorces would be a thing of the past.

Selfless. Simply think about your spouse and support him before you do yourself. It sends a strong message that you care and value your spouse. It is also selfish of the husband or wife to bring baggage into the marriage without discussing the issue with the other spouse. Several things such as trust issues can create a very challenging relationship that could result in separation or divorce. Remember not to take each other for granted. We tend to treat the world ten times better that the ones who love you and who will stand by you no matter what. In order words, we put on a show for the world, but behind closed doors there is another person that is revealed. Each person in the relationship should be treated as if they are the queen and king. You each deserve it. You know "Joy", unspeakable "Joy". That's what you want in your relationship.

It's Not How You Start
Kawaniee Flowe

Not every wife reading this book is in a marriage that started in a godly manner. Many of us,

truth be told, can look back and admit that instead of having GOD at the foundation, we were

wooed by sex, money, status, looks, loneliness, or any number of worldly influences. In reality,

the way things began inevitably had a lasting impact on how you have proceeded. But, take joy,

my sisters. Even if you didn't begin your marriage with a godly focus, you have the power and authority to make some changes today [2 Peter 1:3, Luke 10:19]. How you started is not how you have to continue. There is a GOOD BOOK (other than this one) that will give you some instructions on how to set your marriage on the right path! The institution of marriage was created and established by God [Gen. 2:18, 21-25]. So, if you are not including The Creator in the process, it is going to be very difficult to fully experience marriage in the way it was planned. God established the covenant between a man and a woman and declared that the two shall become one flesh [Genesis 2:21-25, Matthew 19:5, Mark 10:8, Ephesians 5:31]. Now, in order for us to restore proper order to our marriages, and experience that oneness, we must look to the Word of God and apply what it instructs. Two of the clearest instructions we find in the Bible are for a man to love his wife and for a wife to RESPECT her husband [Ephesians 5:33]. Since this book is specifically for wives, we will focus on our instruction to respect our husbands. This is a HUGE and challenging area to develop, especially if it wasn't established prior to marriage. Now, before we go any further with how to show respect, we should take an honest assessment of what we know about it. It is impossible to give something that we don't clearly understand. There is a reason that we, as women, were specifically directed to respect our husbands. What do we know about respect? Where did we learn about it? How did we apply it before our marriage? These are all questions we must consider as we seek to make it a part of our all day, every day role as a wife. Believe it or not, a great place to evaluate your personal understanding of respect is to reflect on your past. Everyone may have a different story, but, if this is not your first marriage, or if your husband was not your first sexual partner, the biblical truth is the same. Now, my prayer is that you are reading this with an open heart and an open mind, ready to face the TRUTH, embrace the TRUTH and be restored by the TRUTH. Respect starts within you. How you have been given respect and how you have shown respect to yourself. You see, it is nearly impossible to give properly, something that you have never received properly. So, consider this for a moment... before you met and married your husband, how well did you respect yourself? Did you treat your body as the temple that it is [1 Corinthians 6:18-20]; the temple that was created in the image of GOD [Genesis 1:27]. Some of us did not. The reasons may vary, but the end result is the same. Many of us entered our marriages after having allowed our bodies to be misused, abused and disrespected at length and carry very deep scars. You see, whether you realize it or not, a part of you that should have been sacredly reserved for your husband, was already violated. It may have been by choice, through a promiscuous lifestyle, it may have been by through unfortunate circumstances, situations and experiences, it may have even been through good intentions that resulted in bad results. Regardless of how unholy copulation came about, it has inevitably left a mark. Every failed relationship, in some way, has impacted our self-respect and for some of us, our general ability to respect men. We carry bits and pieces of hurt with us that spring up, any time they aggravated. Dr. Edmond Locard, a forensic scientist puts this in perspective with a statement known as the Locard's exchange principle: "Every contact leaves a trace[https://en.wikipedia.org/wiki/Locard%27s_exchange_principle]. This means that in the world of forensics, there is a belief that no person can enter a room without leaving physical evidence of having been there. Now consider that theory on an emotional level. Imagine someone who has been joined to you in an intimate fashion, such as sexually, and consider the lingering emotional evidence. For some of us, this is a distressing thought to consider. However, thank God we are blessed with a greater biblical truth. Christ is not only our Savior; He is also our RESTORER [Titus 3:3-7]!

Everything you could ever want to know about your restoration can be found in the Word of God and if you let it, that Word will restore you from the inside in order for it to be manifested through you on the outside. No matter what state of brokenness you may have been in at the beginning of your marriage or may be in now, God can do a work in you to restore both you and your marriage. As God begins a work in you, He can use you to win over and restore your husband's love for you and for God [1 Peter 3:1-6]. So what do you do if you believe your marriage has already been irreparably damaged by overwhelming disrespect or a lack of love? Go deeper! Go harder! And Study longer! This is still for you, regardless of whether it causes a change in your husband. If by chance it doesn't change your husband's heart, the work that God can do in you through His Word will be useful to restore you spiritually. If your marriage is struggling, you need the Word of God to

69

strengthen it. If your marriage is healthy and thriving, you need the Word of God to sustain it. If you are already separated, physically or emotionally, in your marriage, you need the Word of God to restore it. Whatever condition your marriage is in, you need the Word of God—not just for your marriage, but for you. If you study it and apply it, the Word can work in you and through you [2 Timothy 3:16-17]. Don't despair and don't be discouraged, because the start of a thing does not have to dictate how it ends [Ecclesiastes 7:8, Isaiah 43:19]. Along with the Word, pray for your marriage, pray for your spouse, and pray for yourself. Pray, pray and pray! The Bible says pray without ceasing [1 Thessalonians 5:16-18]. I have a challenge for you. Consider all of the married couples you know. Ask the wives if they pray for their husbands daily. Do you SEE any differences between the marriages that have praying wives? Do you see any difference in the women who pray? How about you? Who do you talk to about your situation? Is it your girlfriend who doesn't have a godly man in her life, your married friend who is miserable in her marriage, or do you stay silent and worry alone? Try talking to God about your situation. He is always available. Even when He is silent, He is listening and considering your needs Consider this—Jesus Himself intercedes for us [Hebrews 7:25, Romans 8:34]. Now keep in mind that your prayers must be pure. Do NOT ask God to rain down fire and brimstone on the head of your unloving husband, but offer prayers for correction and restorations in your marriage to the glory of God [Philippians 4:4-7]. We were created to have dominion over the earth [Genesis 1:26-28]. That dominion cannot be taken away; it has to be relinquished. Too many of us are relinquishing our marriages without a fight, and if we are fighting, we are fighting the wrong enemy - with the wrong weapons [Ephesians 6:10-24]. Our husbands are not our enemy! We were given to them as a sacred gift from God to be a suitable helpmate [Genesis 2:18]. How well are you functioning as a gift? Not by a worldly standard, but according to God's plan and purpose for you in the life of your husband. If God were to sit down with you right now, and evaluate you on your performance, what kind of marks would you receive? Consider your thoughts towards your husband. No matter how hard we try, we cannot hide from them and we certainly cannot hide them from God[Psalm 139]. If we want our marriages to be restored and sustained, we have to transform how we think about our husbands [Philippians 4:8-9]. This does not mean you lie to yourself or ignore your husband's shortcomings, but you do not allow them to overshadow the thoughts of him becoming the man that God planned for him to be. God does not gossip. He is not showing you these character flaws for you to condemn him, but to help him. That may be through gently words of encouragement and direction or it may be through silent prayers. Whatever is needed, you need a solid relationship with your husband's Creator to know what you are to do. Do you talk to and about your husband with respect? Remember, God is evaluating you. He knows your thoughts and He hears what comes out of your mouth. What are you speaking over your husband? Speak the Word over him and over your household [Deuteronomy 30: 14-15]. Be wary of disrespectful thoughts and words and do not fall into deception about your own self-righteousness. You are one flesh. What you speak over him will inevitably impact you and your family. Finally, how are you treating him? Even the Bible speaks about the misery of living with a quarrelsome wife [Proverbs 25:24]. Seek to satisfy your husband, both physically and spiritually[Proverbs 5: 19, Proverbs 31]. No matter what has transpired before your marriage or what has transpired during your marriage, that may have challenged it, or even damaged it, you have the opportunity for it to be transformed. Put aside the past and pick up the Good Book to start your journey to the future. Either way, the result is bound to reveal a better you.

Kawaniee "Kay" Flowe is a nurse who retired from the United States Air Force after 27 years of service. She is the wife of 16 years to Charles M. Flowe, Sr. Together they are the proud parents of one son in college and one daughter in elementary school. They are also the co-facilitators of the Love Fellowship Christian Center, Real Love Marriage Ministry. Kay truly loves the Lord and is always willing to share her "2008 Damascus Road Experience" while deployed to Iraq. It was that experience, with God, that changed her heart, her life, and transformed her marriage.

God Allowed Your Union, So You Belong Together
Vivian Strong

My husband, Victor, and I were two strong people who loved each other and wanted to be together. We got married before God, our family, and friends, and both of us thought forever would be automatic. It wasn't long before reality set in. We had lived together for four years before getting married and thought we knew all there was to know about each other. What we did not know was that once you tie the knot, the clock starts over in your relationship, regardless of how long you lived together. This may be a psychological thing, but you don't think like a true married couple until you say, "I do". We were in a committed relationship, but we did not really belong to each other until we made it official. At that point, we became secure in our relationship.

So there we were, newly married, and we began to start seeing behaviors and attitudes in each other that we had not seen before. Our perceptions about marriage did not really reveal themselves until after we were comfortably committed in marriage. Thirty years ago when we got married, there was no real pre-marital counseling, marriage mentors, or other means to prepare us for marriage. We mistakenly thought that we had seen all there was to see while living together during those four years.

We started to see differences in each other, and the differences were a surprise. And surprises in new marriages can become problems if handled incorrectly. Surprises can not only take the form of your previously-unrevealed perceptions, but also the form of other people's attitudes about your marriage and how you handle these people when you encounter them.

For example, Victor and I had different perceptions about the roles of husbands and wives in marriage. My husband was an only child, raised in a household with both his mother and father. His father was the main breadwinner, who led the family. His mother owned and operated a beauty shop, but her first priorities were her husband and son. She cooked, cleaned, and catered to them as such.

My father and grandmother, on the other hand, raised me. Our home was constantly busy with family and people that my grandmother had "adopted" and offered assistance to. We all pitched in and helped with the daily chores and other responsibilities. I did not see the example of husband and wife roles that my husband saw daily. Instead, I saw it from a distance in other outside marriages. Sharing chores, and being considerate, self-sufficient, and independent were part of my daily life.

I did not intimately know a wife to be what my husband thought a wife was. He expected me to know what he knew, and it caused some contention between us. I did not know what to expect, except that we would share. This clashed with my husband's perceptions and expectations. Through trial and error, we were able to come to a meeting of the minds. Once we understood that we each had different perceptions and expectations about our roles as husband and wife, we were able to learn about each other and compromise. We had to figure out what was really important, not just what was habit.

Another example of differing perceptions was between me and my family and friends. My husband was a cook when we met. Now, I had some friends and family that would not have considered him for a relationship because of his job. I saw and fell in love with the man, his values, his character, his heart, and his "real" wealth.

He was a man who loved his family, and this love, consideration, and responsibility for us motivated him to do more to provide for us. In doing more to provide for us, this young husband and father went back to school and became a dietary supervisor, then a dietary manager, and then a food service director. Then he made a career change to food and equipment sales and had a great career. He desired to provide for us, not just make money, and he did that well. So you see it was not where he was, but where he was going and what fueled him.

When you follow your heart and God, everything else will fall into place. And sometimes this will happen at the expense of other relationships that you have. You will need the courage and strength to stand for each other, despite what others think or feel.

We also handled conflict in our marriage. We differed considerably in how we executed the rules of engagement. I have never been a docile woman. I had my own thoughts and opinions and was always allowed to be expressive. I was a fighter. This was a little more than my husband could handle at first, and it clashed with his perception of a wife, so when we had conflict and I argued with him, he would walk out. The way we were handling conflict almost cost us our marriage. I could not understand why he walked out when upset, and he could not understand why I argued.

We both thought our approaches to conflict were fine. What we later found out, through trial and error, was that my husband was walking away because he was so angry and felt disrespected. I was so angry because he walked away, making me feel abandoned and unloved. These are the worst feelings to have about your spouse. Once we understood the underlying effects of how we handled conflict, we were able to better control our reactions. I made a conscious effort to curb my arguing because I did not want to disrespect my husband. My husband never left the house when angry again once he knew how hurtful it was to me. We both were just doing what we'd always done, but in our marriage, it had devastating effects. We had to learn this and correct it for the sake of our marriage.

Our differences could have destroyed our marriage. Our different expectations and perceptions about marriage were not obvious and the differences subtly undermined oneness in our marriage. They were like the little foxes that destroy the vineyard. Because they were small and seemingly insignificant, the tendency is to ignore and minimize their ability to wreak havoc in our marriages, but that is exactly what they will do if you don't guard against them. It had gotten to a point with us where we were not sure our marriage would make it to the five-year mark. But God had a different plan for us, in spite of us. And we know it was God because many have divorced for some of the same issues that we faced and survived. Every time we wanted to throw in the towel, God redirected us, and we were never able to separate. Here we are at thirty years and still going strong.

Couples today have many resources that were not available to my husband and I. Pre-marital counseling is a must. This can help you to identify your differing perceptions and expectations and help you to handle them better. Mentoring is another great tool available today. Couples who have been married longer can be a great resource and can share how they handle the day-to-day marriage walk. Counseling is there to help when you are at a standstill and can't figure how to make things work. Fellowshipping with other couples and attending conferences and retreats help to keep our marriage strong today and are very necessary in spite of all our years together.

Here is what my husband and I have found: Marriage is like two people each living in separate, fully furnished houses of the same size, who buy a third house that is the same size as the other two, but empty. The couple has to decide which pieces from each of the other two houses will be added to their new house. It sounds easy, but the process can be long and sensitive. That old chair that you think is a piece of junk, she loves because it belonged to her loving Grandmom, who went home to be with the Lord. The old sports shirt that she thinks should be trashed, you've kept because it represents an obstacle that you were able to overcome. You cannot dismiss the things that may be important to your spouse. You must try to understand what it means to the other and weigh its sentimental value to your spouse when making the decision about what to keep.

With time, patience, and understanding, the two of you will painstakingly decide which items from each of your houses (baggage) will go to the new house. Some things will not be going, and it may be a process for your spouse to let these things go. And one day, you will look up and your new house, marriage, is fully furnished with just the right pieces that you both want there.

Jerimiah 29:11 says: "For I know the plans I have for you, declares the Lord, plans to prosper you and not to harm you, plans to give you hope and a future."

Song of Songs 2:15 says: "Catch for us the foxes, the little foxes that ruin the vineyards, our vineyards that are in bloom."

Vivian Strong is a wife, married 30 years, Certified Biblical Counselor, Certified Marriage Mentor, SYMBIS Assessment Analyzer, Sharon Baptist Church Marriage Enrichment Ministry Servant Leader, SBC Deaconess, Certified Mastering the Mysteries of Love Communication Skills Coach, and Accountant of 25 years.

To Love,
Honor,
And
Cherish

A Word From
Coach Da-Nay Macklin

"Wives on Fire" is truly heaven sent...a heavenly haven!

As wives we need a place of refuge, sanctuary, retreat or whatever you want to call it. Having been married for 9 years (together for 16 years) we have been through the good, the bad, and the ugly! Any marriage over the course of time is going to be reflective of the good, the bad, and oh yes it can get ugly. Don't allow the bad and the ugly to deter you from marriage because marriage is truly a beautiful roller-coaster. Just like a roller-coaster, in the beginning of marriage we are cruising upward, the sky is the limit! Then we hit the top only to experience a drop to the bottom. For me that was when adultery shook our marriage to the core! Glory to God he worked that situation out for us. As a result, we have truly experienced "Love after Adultery."

Just like a roller-coaster our marriage smoothed out and we were back on the up and up again only to be hit with some loops, hard turns, and drops followed by a separation that almost ended in divorce. Again I say, Glory to God, as He worked that out for us and can work it out for you too! We are going and growing stronger in our marriage than we ever have before. I wish I would have had "Wives on Fire" to save me from the heartbreak and headaches. This book brings a great deal of comfort in knowing that we as wives are never alone!

Healing comes from the true, real, and raw stories of wives, like myself, who have successfully navigated test after test turning it into a testimonial to triumph while encouraging our other sister wives to do the same. Marriage is a remarkable and beautiful roller coaster that I would ride again and again with my loving and supportive husband as we have confronted and conquered adultery to separation and more. Most importantly, through it all we continue to grow in God and guidance to weather any storm. As we know, after the storm comes a rainbow…reap your harvest through "Wives on Fire"!

Coach Da-Nay Macklin BS, CCLC, author of Love After Adultery: The Breakthrough Journey of the Brokenhearted, has been featured on the Oprah Winfrey Network's show Unfaithful: Stories of Betrayal, after successfully navigating adultery in her marriage. She is one of the nation's leading experts on infidelity recovery and prevention, a certified life coach, empowerment speaker, business coach, and entrepreneur mastermind mentor. She is also the President and Chief Executive Officer of Da-Nay International LLC, located in Charlotte, North Carolina. Contact her at: www.danaymacklin.com

Life Calling
Ciara Desper

It is so much easier to remember the bad experiences in life than the good. I have always had temporary amnesia when it relates to my childhood memories. Amnesia has been my coping mechanism. I call it temporary, because I have continued my journey with the Lord and he has revealed bits and pieces of my past to me over time.

I remember growing up as a very shy and timid person. I never spoke up and was too scared to speak back. It was very easy to run over me and to use me. I wasn't very good in school as a child, and I could only do well enough to pass. I was a "C" student. I also got in trouble a lot, which I now realize was a cry for attention. My mother was on drugs; a crack cocaine addict. My biological father, who was the one who introduced my mother to drugs, was nowhere to be found. I was left to raise myself along with my younger brother and sister in a one-bedroom apartment that we shared with my mother and stepfather. On one side on the room sat my parent's bed, and on the other side of the room was our bunk bed. My sister and I were on the bottom bed and my brother was on the top bed. Numerous events occurred in this apartment which helped shape my life and prepare me for the call God had for me.

Earlier I mentioned that my mother was on drugs. She was very good at hiding it though. Anyone that was not a part of our immediate family couldn't tell she had an addiction. She dressed well and always kept a job. Drugs were her coping mechanism in order to deal with all the hurt and pain she had suffered as a child. Today she has nearly fourteen years of sobriety.

During her years of using drugs I dealt with neglect. However, during her years clean I dealt with the same neglect, but also with physical, mental, and verbal abuse along with her being in and out of jail. She was a retail thief; also known as a booster.

Even though she didn't use drugs anymore during later years, she still had a drug addict mentality. It often seemed like my life had gotten even worse. My mother would beat the hell out me for no reason, until the point when I got older and I started fighting back. I remember going to high school graduation with a busted lip because of her. I was so mad at God at this point in my life. I was always taught to, "Honor thy mother and father," but no one taught the other part; that parents must not provoke their children. She verbalized how she wished she had aborted me and called me all types of names like, "whore, slut, etc." Due to my hate, I became the daughter that said, "I will never be like my mother." Little did I know that her behavior was going to affect me all the way into adulthood, and I became my mother's child.

As a teenager a series of horrible events occurred, and the character I had before then no longer existed. I was outgoing and playful at times, and then at other times I was mean and angry. It felt good to no longer allow people to walk all over me, but over time I became very self-righteous. I would cut class and I fought a lot. I used to love hanging with my friends and I was able to hang with them frequently as long as my brother and sister came along. For this reason, I never wanted children. I felt like a teenage mother. It was so embarrassing, and everyone made fun of me as a result.

During my teenage years I became more independent. I got a job, but because my stepfather always stole my mother's money to support his gambling habit, I was forced to give money to my mom to pay the bills. I got tired of working to give money to my parents, so after a year of working at Burger King I just quit. I was getting used to not having money again but I always wanted nice things. Over time I became a booster like my mother. I tried to stop numerous times, but it was hard. I kept getting caught, but that still didn't stop me. It wasn't until I was 19 when I got caught by authorities after stealing a great deal of merchandise that I was charged with a felony.

I must say now that I thank God for allowing me to get caught. My criminal record no longer allowed me to get any job I wanted, so I decided to go to school for cosmetology. I had always loved doing hair around the neighborhood, but I never saw myself going to school for it or becoming a professional. Today I am a very successful hairstylist. I have worked with many celebrities; I've been in newspapers, on television and even paid to travel to demonstrate hair tools and products. I know I would have never gone to school for hair if the decision was left solely up to me. I had been halfway through a degree in nursing when I got arrested the final time. I am a true believer that all things work together for good, and I was able to see that scripture came into my life through that experience. I have never stolen another piece of merchandise since that day.

You would think that after all those experiences I would follow God, but nope. I didn't. I wanted to have fun. I wanted to party and I wanted to sleep around with my on-again-off-again boyfriend, who is now my husband Avery. It wasn't until fall of 2010 that I went to church with a guy I was dating and he introduced me to Enon. I fell in love with the church, and on November 2nd I received my right hand of fellowship. The day I walked down the aisle to dedicate my life back to God, there was a sermon being taught called, "Discipleship Means Deeper." To me that was not a coincidence. The only person that came to see me that day was my grandmother. My mother was mad at me because I had made the decision to leave our family church.

Once I made the decision to dedicate my life back to God, I felt like all hell broke loose. I couldn't keep a man and all means of income were taken away from me. I lost my apartment and I was stuck sleeping on a sofa in my best friend's room at her parent's house. This was my life for an entire year. In that year I became celibate, I stopped clubbing, I regularly attended church and Bible study, and most importantly in that year I built a relationship with God and I met him for myself. Amen.

"Does he have any money? Does he dress nice, or what can he do for you?" These are the kinds of questions I was asked as a child when I would tell my mother I had a crush on someone. These are the questions I began to ask myself when I was dating different men. I was a gold digger and I was good at it. I used men to fill voids that only God would truly be able to fill. I always had a boyfriend, but I would just lie and cheat to get want I wanted. Then God brought me to a place of submission and took everything from me. Those money hungry days were over. I broke up with my long-term boyfriend Avery and I was man-free for a year. I learned so much about myself during that time, and by the end of the year I was happy and content with being single. I was content with having God, and in this place of contentment my life starting turning around. Avery and I decided to build a friendship again. I was honest with him from the beginning about the new person I had become and where I wanted to go. I laid down the rules; no sex, no living together, and most importantly you must love God. Avery said yes to all my demands. For the first couple months he came to Enon with me and he joined the Young Adult Ministry with me as well. It was a couple of months after coming to church, on a Sunday, that he walked down the aisle to be saved. It was a beautiful moment for me.

Six months after that he asked me to marry him. At first I told him no. I needed to fast and pray, then ask the Lord if this was what he wanted for me. Sure enough, I fasted and prayed, and got the ok from God. Just like that we were engaged. However, all the leaders in the Young Adult Ministry were very mad at us. They thought this was an immature move, since Avery was still a babe in Christ. It was their negative response that actually confirmed God's word for me. If there had not been any type of attack or people coming against what God had told us, I would have been more concerned and wondering if we had made the right decision. At this point of my faith I knew how the enemy worked. When it comes to God blessing me, Satan always uses something or someone to go against God's message for me. The Bible tells us to be aware of the Devil's schemes, and at that moment I was. This was just the first of many occurrences that helped me learn to trust and stand on God's word, and to trust him with our marriage no matter what anyone had to say against it.

Now, at this time life was sweet. I was engaged, I now had an apartment, and I had an awesome job. All of a sudden one of the most life changing events I had thus far with God transpired. Sitting in my room on the floor while doing my hair and makeup, God whispered in my ear and said, "You were molested!" In disbelief, God brought back a memory of what had happened. All of a sudden I remembered it as if it were yesterday. "For 15 years I had no idea. How could I forget that something so terrible had happened to me? How could this have happened to me?" It was all I could think about. When I went to tell Avery what had happen to me, he told me he already knew. Through his experience working with delinquent and abused children he was able to recognize similar behavior in a young student in his school that had been molested as well. For days and nights I cried. That same week one of my old friends from the young adult ministry approached, me asking if I could be her support at a counseling group called SAS, a sexual abuse group conducted at Enon. She had no idea I had been molested as well, therefore I knew God was perfectly orchestrating something.

Once I begin going to the meeting, all type of emotions began to surface. I was mad at everybody, and especially my mother. I felt like she was supposed to protect me and be there for me. I was even mad at God. How could he say he loved me but allow something like this happen to me; a defenseless child? It was in those moments the Holy Spirit would come and comfort me. His presence would ease my mind in its magnitude. I was so weak in those moments, and he became my strength. So many questions were answered about why I did the things that I have done. So many hurtful spirits like lust, trust issues, people pleasing, forgiveness, anger, etc., manifested themselves in my mind as a result of that one act. God began to open my heart and reveal all these things about me, and then he began to help me deal with them.

Molestation was a generational curse in my family. Someone has touched almost every woman in my family unwillingly, whether it was a family member or someone close to the family. Going through the process of healing, I became bold enough to bring the topic up amongst my family. Everyone was very mad at me. You just don't talk about stuff like that in my family. I made a decision that day that this would no longer happen in my family, and that this generational curse ends with me. I didn't realize what I was taking on at the time but I must say today it is worth it. Through the process of healing I was also able to understand my mother more and why she had done the things she did. She was molested multiple times by multiple different men. Sometimes the abuse was caused by the men my grandmother would bring into the house. By trusting God in all his ways and not leaning to my own understanding, I realized that what I went through wasn't just a burden for me to bear, but instead a gift to share. Today I am not just a part of SAS, and my mother now comes with me too. I serve an awesome God. Ephesians 3:20 says, "Now to Him who is able to do exceedingly abundantly above all that we ask or think, according to the power that works in us."

Still only engaged, I was again sitting on the floor in my room doing my hair and makeup in the mirror when I started talking to God. I began by asking him a question I had asked before, only this day he decided to answer me back. I asked, "How are you going to use this marriage for your glory, and what ministry have you called us to?" God responded, "Marriage Ministry." Unlike Samuel, I was familiar with God's audible voice, since that was how He spoke to me often in that particular time of my life. I was excited, but then that excitement soon turned into fear and feelings of inadequacy.

The next day Avery and I had our weekly check-in as usual. He came to me and told me that God spoke to him, that we would be married, and we would work together to help other married couples as a team. It felt so good to see how we were on one accord, and how we could confirm each other's call. A couple days after my God told us our call, you told us to join Exploring Your Call and exactly what track to be a part of. We knew for an entire year what God had called us to do, and what would be our next step. I honestly have no idea how he will bring us together in helping people in marriage since I am on the counseling track and Avery is a part of the teaching track, but I am excited we get to approach marriage ministry from two different perspectives.

From there on Avery and I began to grow even closer together. In 2011, about a month after knowing our call, Avery and I were praying. It was the weekend of The Day of Pentecost. As we were praying, we suddenly began speaking in tongues together! We knew nothing about tongues. I never knew anyone close to me who ever had the gift. As we spoke in tongues, I understood him and he understood me. From that moment on we were moving as one in both the natural world and the realm of the Holy Spirit.

Now married for two years, I know that my God has redeemed me. I was able to marry a man who absolutely loves me, despite my many flaws. He knows about my past and has never judged me. Avery and I are very excited about what God is doing in our lives. We were once a part of the Young Adult Ministry, and now we still interact with them as much as possible. We are now being asked to come talk to other young adults about what it means to be married at a young age, how it's ok to be celibate and how we honor our covenant with God. People our age are seeing the call in our life and I thank God for that. As we attend "Not Easily Broken" every Sunday we get a first-hand look at what it is like to counsel and teach others. We get to learn scriptures about marriage and how to respect one another. We also get to see couples that have been married for 20, 30, and even 40 years and learn from them. Avery and I are currently a part of the Intercessor Ministry. As a child I always admired the mothers in the church that would pray. I always had a heart and a desire to pray. Prayer is a strong part of our marriage today. Every day we pray together, then once a week we fast and we have a check-in where we communicate our issues and express how much we love and appreciate each other. Prayer is what is keeping us working together in this season. Right now I am the financial provider of the household. When we joined EYC my husband lost his job and has no income to contribute. Our financial roles have completely switched. Avery now washes clothes and cooks as I support the household financially; while at the same time respecting and honoring him as the head of the household. The respect part has been easy because I see God's hand in the situation blocking him from being able to get a job. Not being able to always have what I want has been really hard, but I know things will turn around and this too shall pass.

In a couple years I would like to be fully operating in our ministry, but I'm not sure if that will happen. God hasn't revealed it all to me yet. He deals with me one step at a time, and I love it that way. If I know too much I will try to get ahead of him. I would personally like to travel around the world helping couples one marriage at a time, in Jesus name. For now I see us staying local and helping our young adult population. I think they will respond to us well. One thing I know is that people don't want you talking "At" them but "With" them. Their struggles are our struggles, and we are more relatable to them than an elderly couple who might have no idea what is really going in our generation.

I thank God for all my trials and tribulations. I thank him for the process I am currently going through. I know that I was called before I entered my mother's womb, and my life is perfectly orchestrated for what he has called me to do (Jeremiah 5:1). My experiences while being abused, molested, and taken advantage of did not feel good. It hurt me very badly, but I serve a God that can take the pain away. I serve a God that can deliver and heal. I serve a God that would never leave me nor forsake me. Today I no longer am a victim, I am the victor! I now have a wonderful, intelligent, and gorgeous husband who loves me for who I am and all my mess too! I don't think people fully understand what marriage means to God, and I want them to understand. The freedom, the deliverance, the love I have in God, and the love I have for my husband are all things I want for other women to experience. I want to see marriages restored and families back together. Most of all I want to hear, "Well done thy good and faithful servant," from my Father's mouth. Amen.

Ciara Desper is a Licensed Cosmetologist, celebrity hairstylist, and student residing in the southern area of New Jersey. She and her husband, Avery, met on June 23, 2003 while both attended Willingboro High School. As high school sweethearts, their love and courtship continued up to the time they became engaged. They were joined together in Holy Matrimony on February 10, 2013.

Currently, Ciara is pursuing a Bachelor of Science in Psychology at Wilmington University and interning for Life After Trauma Organization (LATO), an organization that helps women recover from trauma resulting from human trafficking. Along with her husband, she is pursuing a Certificate of Biblical Studies at Palmer Seminary in Pennsylvania while she practices as a celebrity hair stylist.

Ciara is an innovative hair stylist with an eye for trendy,

cutting edge, new styles. She has been styling hair for more than 10 years and has worked with a wide range of clients - from celebrities such as Elle Varner, YaYa Dacosta, and Robin Givens; to also serving as an official hair stylist of the Philadelphia 76ers; to the everyday woman and children of all ethnic backgrounds and cultures. She was also featured in the Philadelphia Inquirer.

As a married couple, Avery and Ciara's mission is to have a marriage that is centered on the teachings and work of Jesus Christ, which they hope ultimately brings glory to God. Through their dedication to their spiritual life in Christ, it is their desire to be obedient servants, exemplifying the grace of God. Through their collective ministry, Ciara and Avery's vision is to create a counseling environment that both educates and enlightens others through shared experiences and their understanding on how to build a healthy marriage- one that is worthy to give back to God.

Ciara supports her husband in his role as Assistant Servant leader of Enon Tabernacle Baptist Church's "Not Easily Broken" marital enrichment ministry.

~ Her Wife Verse ~

She does him good, and not harm, all the days of her life. Proverbs 31:12

Communication
Eve Harmon

SEX AND INTIMACY

The art of marriage is the ability to communicate effectively with your spouse. Marriages are falling apart because of infidelity, finances, and boredom, which results in a breakdown of communication.

We go outside of marriage to fill a lonely space. Perhaps it is the lack of sex; the sex is too scripted, or the sex is just not good. At one point, the sex was so good when you were in a courtship with your spouse (assuming you were not born again Christians during that season). You were probably sexing each other all night long and every chance you could get, right? Wives you probably were going to bed smelling good with your silk lingerie and hair tossed-up, right? So what happened? Why have you become so lazy in the area of sexing your husband? You are forcing him to go outside of your marriage. You might-as-well auction him off to the nearest homewrecker. Are you that oblivious that you think your Christian husband's flesh will not become weak, and he will not seek satisfaction elsewhere? Wives, it is your duty to have sex with your husband; the Bible says, *"Now concerning the matters about which you wrote: "It is good for a man not to have sexual relations with a woman." But because of the temptation to sexual immorality, each man should have his own wife and each woman her own husband. The husband should give to his wife her conjugal rights, and likewise the wife to her husband. For the wife does not have authority over her own body, but the husband does. Likewise the husband does not have authority over his own body, but the wife does. Do not deprive one another, except perhaps by agreement for a limited time, that you may devote yourselves to prayer; but then come together again, so that satan may not tempt you because of your lack of self-control". 1 Corinthians 7:1-5*

Satan may tempt your husband to go outside of the marriage. His lack of self-control boils down to a breakdown in your communication. Ask yourself, how many times has your husband requested for you to come to bed looking a certain way and smelling good? Once a request is verbalized, it becomes a form of communication. Wives, we can be so wrapped up in our spirituality that we lose focus and believe that since our husbands are devoted to the word of GOD, he won't become weak to another women's flesh. That women's flesh is satan undercover, trying to break the bricks that hold the foundation to your marriage. Then you ask yourself, why is this happening to me? It may be happening because you didn't listen or hear your husband's cry. You ignored his request for a particular look or smell. You shut down the communication. Why? Because of your obtuse thinking that satan didn't know there was a breakdown of communication in your marriage (sex life), and he found a way to dismantle your vows.

So wives, my charge to you is to go on a shopping spree for lingerie. You might be saying, "Yeah, right, where am I going to find the money for lingerie?" I'm so glad you asked. The amount of money you're spending on unnecessary items each month could be used to buy some sexy lingerie. It's worth the investment of honoring your husband's request and by listening to his needs, you can prevent or to stop the infidelity in your marriage and work on building your communication skills.

FINANCE

Finance....finance...finance can destroy our happy home. Why? We're under the assumption that our spouse is paying our bills, until the car is repossessed, the credit cards have been declined, or you receive a shut-off notice for a utility bill. Why live by an assumption when you can communicate about your monthly finances?

First, there should be only one CFO (Chief Financial Officer) to avoid chaos or unnecessary arguments. You should have one account for the household expenses and an individual account for yourself. In my case, I keep it simple by writing my CFO (my husband) a personal check towards our monthly expenses. You might be asking, how do I know my hubby is taking care of business? We communicate about our finances by having monthly financial meetings, so we're both are on the same page. We both have a checking account, a saving account, and individual retirement funds (which we do not touch), as well as joint credit cards. We also have emergency funds. We do not use our credit cards without consulting with each other and come up with a plan to pay the credit card bill. This is a traditional set up and is not popular but it works for hubby and me.

So wives, do what works for you. My charge to you is to communicate regarding your finances monthly, so both parties are aware of what's going. Live within your means; the Bible said, *"Therefore do not be anxious, saying, 'What shall we eat?' or 'What shall we drink?' or 'What shall we wear?' For the Gentiles seek after all these things, and your heavenly Father knows that you need them all. But seek first the kingdom of God and his righteousness, and all these things will be added to you. "Therefore do not be anxious about tomorrow, for tomorrow will be anxious for itself. Sufficient for the day is its own trouble. Matthew 6:31-34*

And my God will supply every need of yours according to his riches in glory in Christ Jesus. Philippians 4:19

You should order a credit report every quarter or at least once a year. You're entitled to a free credit report annually from Experian, TransUnion, and Equifax. Utilize the free services. My credit report is a direct reflection that hubby is taking care of business. A good CFO sets financial goals and my husband's financial goal is to be debt-free in 3-years to position us for retirement. What is your financial goal? Do you have a CFO? Do you have monthly financial meetings? These are ways of communicating to alleviate financial trouble in your marriage.

BOREDOM

Is your marriage as spicy as when you courted one another? If not, is it the lack of time, the kids taking up your spare time, or is it just being lazy. Well, it is important that you share the same excitement in marriage that you shared when you were dating.

Do you have date nights? You should date your spouse weekly without outside interference, which means no cell phones. If your phone rings, do not answer it, turn it off, or silence it. Please do not bankrupt yourselves by going out to 5-star restaurants on a weekly basis. You can have a simple date by going to the mall, the movies, bike riding, and long car rides without the radio, or an in-house date. Set your home up as a restaurant, the ambiance should be romantic. Give your restaurant a fictitious name and be your husband's server. Dress up or dress less (lingerie). Afterwards, don't end the date. Dance for your hubby, caress him, and make love to him. Show him your alter-ego in the bedroom. You can also do something different like sexting. The day of your date send your spouse a graphic text (mindful that it goes to the right person) with an itinerary of what your date night looks like. That keeps the spice up by turning it up.

Boredom is another cause of failed marriages. If your spouse is saying we never do the things that we used to do, and it's always the same old thing, translation I am bored in our relationship. This can become an open door for him to seek excitement somewhere else. The Bible says, *"Run from anything that stimulates youthful lust. Instead, pursue righteous living, faithfulness, love, and peace. Enjoy the companionship of those who call on the Lord with pure hearts."* 2 Timothy 2:23

Wives, my charge to you is to listen and observe your husband. Don't take your husband's boredom for granted; especially if he is communicating there is a problem that needs to be addressed.

Lastly, stay in the Word, pray together, and have weekly devotions. Walk by faith, not by sight and this will enhance your communication skills. This chapter was designed to improve the communication skills in your marriage. It takes 21-days to form a habit, so my charge to you is to take these tools and work on your communication skills. It's worth the investment of maintaining and saving our marriage.

The Wife After God's Own Heart: The Proverbs 31 Wife

On 19 May 2001, I married my best friend, Will. The truth of the matter, I did not want to become a wife nor a mother. Nonetheless, God has a way of throwing us curve balls. When I laid eyes on Will, I prophesized that he'll become my husband. As a result of our unity, God has blessed with a bonus son. Furthermore, we are co-parents to my nieces and nephews.

My dedication is to God, and my family who have driven me to work harder to reach my goals. I am following God's vision and walking in his pathway that he has carved out for me. Thus, the road is not easy but when it is God's vision, there would be bumps and bruises along the way. My faithfulness to God has made me a wiser wife. As a result, my husband has confidence in me and my decision making. Indeed, Will's trust and confidence in me represents my symbolic walk with Christ. Through Christ, I am filled with graciousness and wiliness to help others and minister to them as often as I can....

My favorite Bible verse is 2 Corinthians 5:7

Eve Harmon has earned an Associate Degree in Criminal Justice from Community College of Philadelphia, along with a Bachelor's Degree in Organizational Management from Eastern University. Eve is working towards her Master's Degree in Forensic Psychology at Walden University. She is currently a Logistics Specialist for The Department of Defense.

In March 2013, Eve received a plaque from The Defense Logistics Agency, Troop Support Federal Women's Program and Federally Employed Women, "Women of The Year Award". For her dedication and hard work on her job; for her strong family base, and her community outreach.

Eve has an intense passion for outreach; she serves on two ministries at her church, Enon Tabernacle Baptist Church (The Nursing Home Ministry and The Couple Fellowship Ministry). She also serves on the Broad of Directors for True Way Youth Empowerment Foundation, a non-profit organization that empowers our youth with academic, social-emotional, and physical well-being needs through a series of workshops.

Eve is a Licensed Wife's Coach with a concentration in Communication. She believes the key to successful marriage is

Communication. In May 2001, Eve married her best friend, Willie; she has a bonus son and is actively involve in the upbringing of her great-nieces and nephews. When Eve is not taking classes, doing outreach, or spending time with her family, she enjoys spending time alone. She calls, "ME Day" - where she spends a day alone doing her favorite things such as reading, shopping, and reflecting on what's God's next mission for her.

From Friends to Blended
Jocelyn Thorpe

My husband Michael and I met at the age of 15. We were both summer youth employees in an area called "The Bottom" in Philadelphia. One day, while working my summer youth job, on my lunch break, I stood in line at Mimo's Pizza and Michael walked in and picked up the tab. I thought to myself, "Who is this guy? What a smooth gesture."

Unfortunately for him, I already had a high school sweetheart. Michael was persistent, so we became really good friends, so much so that I attended his college graduation in South Dakota. I remember when he called to invite me, his offer to me was that he would fly me out to South Dakota and put me up in a hotel because he wanted his friend to be in attendance for his graduation and he knew that I couldn't afford it.

Days later, he followed the initial offer up with "Would you mind driving 2,400 miles with my parents and I'll take care of your hotel stay?" So I rode with his parents, who I met when they picked me up for the trip. When we arrived in South Dakota, Michael asked me if I could afford to pay for my own hotel. I knew then that I could never date this guy. Was he serious?

Our journey has not been a straight path, but fortunately for us, it led us to matrimony. When we started our relationship, we were mentally battered and abused from both of our first tumultuous marriages.

Our paths took a detour. My first marriage should have never taken place. We were definitely unequally yoked with two opposing value systems. It was really baptism by fire. My mother tried to warn me. She knew his family ran a speakeasy and knew about his upbringing and that it was not conducive to the lifestyle that she envisioned for her child. But guess who thought she was up for the challenge? Me.

It wasn't long before his lies and infidelity consumed me, and I felt like I was drowning. One night after my grandmother, who co-parented me along with my mother, had recently passed, I lost my job, my car broke down, and I found out that my husband had a work mistress and that she was pregnant with his child. I remember feeling like I had hit rock bottom. I knew that God had a much better plan for my life. I wandered into a local church because I had moved away from my home church. All I knew was that I needed to hear a word from God. I distinctly remember praying to God to remove my desire for that man. By this time, I am not even sure why I still had any desire. My commitment to the marriage may have been me personally attempting to avoid the stigma of a failed marriage. The next day, I woke up healed...the desire was gone. Won't He do it? I believe this is when I found my life verse, Jeremiah 29:11, "For I know the plans I think towards you, says the Lord, thoughts of peace and not evil, to give you a future and a hope."

Michael and I were always friends, and he was experiencing his own personal hellacious marriage. Our marital situations ended around the same time. When we started our journey, it was definitely premature. We had so much baggage that some healing time was definitely in order. The issues from our previous relationships surfaced almost immediately. Our blended family situation required much prayer and counseling for all parties involved. Unfortunately, we did not do it.

I have learned that children yearn to be with the absent parent, regardless of the situation. Our relationship in the beginning was difficult at best. It's hard to trust and have an open heart after being betrayed. The fact that we had an established friendship and we knew each other gave us a fighting chance, but believe me, it was rough. The Michael that I knew had always been nice, strong, and respectful, but I think his first marriage had taken a toll on him as mine had.

I remember us encouraging each other. Michael always reminded me about the time that I told him that he had such a talent and that if he used it for something positive, he would be unstoppable. He said that hearing that from me helped him redirect his life. He is now an Executive Director of a multi-million dollar project and a developer. I know there is a God because I know that he prayed for the opportunity and believed. It is amazing see who he has become.

I realize now through study that marriage is a perpetual blend and that our frames of reference were already established. We needed to be molded and shaped so that we could develop a healthy, long-standing relationship. God's Word had to be the source of our molding and shaping.

I grew up in church, so I continued to go. I would often invite Michael to accompany me, but at the time, he wasn't interested. He grew up in church and had to attend three to four nights a week and was "churched out."

One Sunday, after much asking we visited a church in Delaware, The Resurrection Center, which is now our home church. The pastor's message met Michael where he was, and after a few months of visiting, he walked the aisle. After that, we started going to Bible study and we became full-fledged members.

We went through premarital counseling and got married at our church. This is a poem that I wrote for our wedding:

"We started down low, down the bottom, you see. I was a summer youth worker and he a ghost employee. Some of the details are fuzzy and they run amuck. There were some Murjani jeans, a pizza, and he drove an orange truck. We became very good friends over time, but the thought of a relationship never entered my mind. Our lives took a detour and things just weren't right, so I prayed for some joy for the rest of my life. We reunited as friends and our friendship was true, and it led us here to this altar, God, thanks to You.

After we were married, we joined the marriage ministry and eventually became leaders. We invited God into our marriage as the third strand to keep us together. We recognized through study that our love languages are different, so we constantly aspire to meet the other's language. Michael's love language is a combination of personal touch and devotion, and my language is a combination of gifts and quality time. Like any other marriage, we have our issues. The difference in our marriage now is that we are certain that our covenant is with God. Our values are consistent and we are certain that with God, our marriage can overcome all obstacles.

During our marriage, we raised our daughter from Michael's first marriage, and God blessed us with a son after years of infertility issues. God has allowed us to become entrepreneurs and given us flexibility so that we can serve our church and the community. It's amazing when you see God's Word reveal itself. God has a plan for all of us. I had to go through the things that I did so that I would learn to depend on and trust in God.

I have learned a lot in my journey. God's Word has helped to remove my blinders. We cannot afford to lean on our own understanding. A lot of the pain and suffering that I was subjected to could have been avoided. The signs were there, but I did not have an ear to hear the truth. Everything that I've gone through was for a purpose. My husband is now an elder and I serve as a deacon. God continues to use us to guide and assist other couples.

I can relate to Abigail in the Bible (1 Samuel 25). She married her first husband, Nabal, who was crude and disrespectful and could not appreciate the good thing that God blessed him with. He mistreated her, but she still covered him. Then God removed him from her life and blessed her with David as her husband. She poured into David, preventing him from making a bad decision that could have negatively blemished his record. David never forgot Abigail's words of encouragement.

Jocelyn Thorpe is a Realtor with Keller Williams Media in Media, PA.

She is licensed in both Pennsylvania and Delaware and works primarily with first time home buyers and investors. Prior to becoming a realtor, Jocelyn worked as a property manager for over 10 years, managing family and senior citizen housing complexes. Jocelyn received her bachelor's degree from Temple University. Before graduating from Temple, she had already discovered her real estate investing interest.

What began as an ambitious school project about income properties, developed into a unique and strategic business. Now 20 years later, Jocelyn and her husband have established their own real estate portfolio of investment properties with many tenants.

Jocelyn later obtained her Master's Degree in Business from Wilmington University. Jocelyn, alongside her husband, was ordained a Deacon at the Resurrection Center in Wilmington Delaware. There she also served in a leadership capacity in the Marriage Ministry. Jocelyn is also a Certified Event and Wedding Coordinator with her own company "An Event to Remember". She serves as her church's Wedding Planner and is responsible for coordinating and overseeing weddings and receptions held at the church. She also implemented an Etiquette program at the church and other venues.

Jocelyn enjoys, traveling, exercising, bowling, and spending quality time with family and friends. Jocelyn's greatest passions are God, her husband, Michael Thorpe, and their children.

Her Life verse is Jeremiah 29:11, "For I know the plans that I have for you," says the Lord. "They are plans for good and not for evil, to give you a future and a hope."

Are You a Builder or a Bulldozer?
Keisha Brown

Have you ever felt that your husband is capable of elevating to the next level, but needed "real talk" from you because he wasn't moving fast enough? Your "real talk" is necessary according to who you or your husband? Do you think making light of what he is not doing is effective? Maybe it's time to change your approach by focusing on the God in your husband and being obedient to God's word.

Wives, we have the power to build him up or tear him down. It is clear that if we are not committed to affirming our faith in his abilities, no one else's opinion matters. This is great news validating the trust and faith our husbands have in us. This means our thoughts of him are well-respected and have great influence. How we use this influence can be seen in his motivation. It can be the key to his greatness or not. If we focus on his faults, it can kill his spirit and want to grow. We as wives have to be obedient to God's word regarding being thankful. Thankfulness is powerful because God is the father who knows how to give good gifts (Matthew 7:11). "In everything give thanks for this is the will of God in Christ Jesus for you" (1 Thessalonians 5:18). This spirit of thankfulness allows us to see the God in our spouse—see his potential for greatness as opposed to his faults. God expects us to love our husbands as He has loved us. In doing so, that love becomes infectious. It can overrule your focus on his faults. 1 John 4:4 says "Greater is He that is in me than he that is in the world". I can do all things through Christ who strengthens me (Philippians 4:13).

Ephesians 3:20 says "Now to him who is able to do immeasurably more than all we ask or imagine, according to His power that is at work within us."

So, wives the next time your lips form to give that "real talk" aka something belittling, think....you are casting doubt on God's word and its power. Who are we to speak against our Father in Heaven? God will hold us responsible for another's fall or rebellion against Christianity. Are we causing our husbands to rebel by nagging? Don't take part in Apostasy like Judas being a conditional Christian. Pray with authority in private and in the presence of our husbands. That is modeling the Christian way right? The difficult part for us after that is just to be quiet and wait on God. Here is where discipline and obedience come in, so let me reiterate. Be quiet and wait. Amen to that!

Sometime as wives we want to inundate God with requests about our husbands. We normally do this from the perspective of what is important to us. Yup, that's selfish, manipulative and domineering. That is the spirit of Jezebel. We have to submit to serving God first before we can submit to our husbands. It's this submission that makes room for us to be the wife God called us to be. I am sure some of this humors God, but some also angers Him. He has made us helpmates. We were called to be a loving partner to our husbands. Although we are probably in a good position to be Director of King Building, God has not given us this title or authority. We are expected to help build. Say it with me, "I am not the boss!"

Philippians 4:6 says, "Be anxious for nothing; but in everything by prayer and supplication with Thanksgiving let your request be made known unto God and the peace of God, which passes all understanding will guard your hearts and minds in Christ Jesus." We must take to the Lord our God our concerns and truly leave them there. Be watchful however of those requests that focus solely on the faults of others and not yours. The constant "reality checks" or "real talk" we think we need to dish out based on what we perceive as our husband's faults or failures can cause resentment. This resentment may drive your husband into the warm arms of another woman. Think about it…if you felt that you could do nothing right for your husband, wouldn't you give up trying at some point? This will be the woman that lends her ear to his problems. He will confide in her instead of you.

She will build him instead of bulldozing. She may speak softly and gently to talents or potential. On the other hand, she may speak rough or tough, appealing to his ego. This woman will make void all the blood, sweat, and tears that you poured into your marriage over the years. Just ponder that for a moment. That is long enough! Wives, don't send your husbands into the wilderness unfed. Open your minds! A good feeding is not limited to sex. Sex is only part of the intimacy we share with our husbands. We must stay intimately connected to him to keep his heart. God must be in the center. Who are we anyway to make light of one's faults? We all have sinned and fall short of God's glory (Romans 3:23).

So wives, we must be specific about our cares when we pray. Let our prayers however, come from a place of gratitude to God. For instance, thank God for a husband that is a good provider, confident, and whose love is exclusively your own. We often want others to change. Consider asking God to change us to be a wife that inspires and one that a husband praises (Proverbs 31:28). Have you ever considered including this in your prayer to God? God, please keep our attraction and wish to be intimate exclusive to one another. In other words, put a word on it in faith not in doubt or in fear. Matthew 21:22 says, "And in all things, whatsoever ye shall ask in prayer believing, ye shall

111

receive." Life and death are in the power of the tongue (Proverbs 18:21). If we change how we encourage our husbands in prayer, we can help transform the situation. This is so even when what we prayed for has yet to happen. Thanking God in good times and bad shows we trust Him with everything. Romans 8:28 says all things work together for good to those who love God, to those who are called according to His purpose.

Wives, encouragement is not reflective on our husbands past. Don't continue to make light of what he used to do in the past if you said you forgave him and promised to move past it. Don't make comparisons on what you would do versus what he should have done. That is not encouraging.

Wives, we already know we are pretty gifted in the multitasking department. Venus, Mars, etc......we are different. Sometimes we forget that fine detail. That is why God gave us to him...to help. Right?

Right now God, I thank you for allowing me the freedom to express my thoughts. It is my prayer that it inspires and enlightens Christian wives. I pray it armors us in the face of adversity in our marriage. Help us Lord to be wives not knives. Hold us accountable, convict us, and bind our tongues to keep from saying hurtful words. Help us to create a home life for him that is nurturing and supportive. Help us create an environment that appeals and encourages his spiritual relationship with God. Help us enhance intimacy in our relationship. Form a hedge around our union keeping us exclusive one to another. Our relationship should be so intimately and spiritually deep that we can think of one another and have peace despite the greatest trouble. The connection we have with our husbands should make them feel they can conquer the world every day. Even when the world beats them up...just knowing what is at home awaiting them. Thank God for a "God given help mate."

Writing this piece has reaffirmed for me the importance of speaking a word over your cares, husband and wife praying together, being obedient to your word, and being a true living testament of Christianity. None of this can happen without knowing God. You can't ride someone else's coat tails into heaven. You must know him for yourself. God I seek a deeper relationship with you more now than ever before. I want to be the wife that builds my husband. I want God to use me. Help my husband become the King and for me to become the Queen you intended us to be.

Wives, I have a very important question to ask you. Are you a builder or a bulldozer?

Submission Starts in the Garden
LaQuita Mason Brown

"And the rib or part of his side which the Lord God had taken from the man, He built up and made into a woman, and He brought her to the man." Genesis 2:22

In the beginning:

In the beginning, I was beyond excited to join my husband in a holy ceremony in the garden with little understanding of what part of Ephesians 5:31 meant:

"The two shall become one flesh."

Although my husband and I were mature believers, I struggled with submission in the beginning of my marriage. I had unknowingly developed an ungodly stronghold in my mind concerning headship over the course of my childhood which then carried over into my marriage. This stronghold not only created a war within, but it was governing my marriage.

Yes, the husband is given the command to love his wife as Christ loves the church, but even the most patient and loving husband will find it difficult to love a wife whose mouth is untamed and demands to be the headship indirectly. Unfortunately, I found myself resembling this wife. It was during the fusion process of becoming one flesh that I realized my flesh did not like the idea of submitting to a male figure. Mind you, I had been in the military for seven years and I never operated in rebellion towards any authoritative figure in the past. However, the revealing of the stronghold was not exposed until the fusing process of becoming one flesh with my husband.

Wives, I have to tell you, I absolutely hated the process and the Jezebel spirit was fortified in my mind. I would think to myself, "Who does this guy think he is?" The giant in me would rise up and war against the gift I prayed for during my single season. The Holy Spirit politely informed me that my rebellion in submitting to my husband was a reflection of my rebellion in submitting to Christ. Wives, can't nobody check you like Holy Spirit can through a type of love that will cause you to get on your face to repent in order for you to be aligned with the original plan and purposes of God concerning the covenant in the garden.

The Holy Spirit is truly the Comforter and the Guide that will lead you into all truth if you allow Him when you are out of order in any area of your life! The enemy will attack marriages in any number of ways because he understands God's mind concerning marriage and the power of a husband and wife in agreement on one accord. He attacked me in the area of submission because he knew this was the one place that would keep my husband and I out of the garden!

The Attack Starts in the Garden:

Oftentimes, I've noticed the enemy attacks me first as the wife through my appetite (my flesh) as he did with Eve. Genesis 3:1 says:

"Now, the serpent was more subtle and crafty than any living creature of the field which the Lord God had made, and he [Satan] said to the woman, 'Can it really be that God has said you shall not eat from every tree of the garden?'"

Notice that the enemy lures Eve out of the presence of her husband during his strategy to tempt her because he understands the power in headship through Adam. Because Eve is not submitted to the headship, the serpent senses that she has not crucified her flesh and he knows he has legal permission to entice her flesh because she is illegally outside of the presence of God and her submitted husband.

The enemy uses the same strategy he used on Eve through the wife because he understands it's through her rebellion against submission that will cause her husband to lose his place in the garden. Wives, we must stay in the garden because that's where we find the presence of a holy God!

Only in the Garden:

Only in the Garden does the husband receive the mind of Christ. Satan understands the power of oneness with the husband, the wife, and Christ through the connection in the garden. He understands that the flesh is non-existent and it's only through the Spirit we are able to abide with the father in the garden. It's only in the garden that God is able to place the submitted husband in a deep sleep in order to pull life out of him and then breathe the breath of life in the very thing he pulled out of him. It's only through our submission as the wife that we experience the unity God intended for us to experience in the garden. Remember. . . Adam was already submitted to God before Eve was ever a physical manifestation.

Satan understands that the woman's submission is a typology of her submitting herself to Christ, and through her submission, Christ reveals to her His mind. It's in the garden that her spirit is strengthened and empowered to speak only the Word, "It is written," and it causes the kingdom of darkness to flee!

Adaptation to Submission in the Garden:

When God had Eve in mind for Adam, he created her to adapt to Adam as he was submitted to God. Genesis 2:18 says:

"Now the Lord said, 'It is not good (sufficient, satisfactory) that the man should be alone; I will make him a helper (suitable, adapted, complementary) for him.'"

117

Wives, God's original plan never included us as the headship in the covenant of marriage. We were designed to be the helpmeet in our husband's life. Fulfill this great assignment through prayer, as your husband is accountable through his submission to God. Encourage, affirm, and aid in your husband's development as the head as he fulfills God's promise concerning marriage.

Satan knows that when a husband and wife are of one accord in the garden, they become a threat to thwart and overthrow the kingdom of darkness!

During pre-marital counseling and the courtship, many of us thought we understood what Paul meant in Ephesians 5:22:

"Wives, be subject (be submissive and adapt yourselves) to your own husbands as [a service] to the Lord."

Many of us are able to quote this text with ease, but it's a completely different experience when you have to actively live SUBMISSION on a daily basis and the Amalekite spirit (your flesh) doesn't want to submit to AUTHORITY in the form of your husband. However, this text really shows you who you are and your reverence towards God.

The text doesn't say submit to your husband as if he were God, but as a service to God. It simply means for us to submit ourselves to our husbands as our husbands submit themselves to God. Wives, this is the order for God's idea of marriage. We don't have the authority to change the order because we feel like we should or we have a better way of doing something.

It's easier to submit to the mind of Christ than trying to do things our way. His way eliminates unnecessary chaos and strife in our marriage! When we stir up conflict in this area, we are simply telling God, "I don't trust you to be the head in my life." When you renew your mind according to God's Word, it's easier to submit to the man of God in your life. Let God be God and allow God to display who He is through the submission of your husband's life.

Instead of being in constant warfare with your husband in this area, be in prayer concerning his position as the head and ask God to give him revelation so that your marriage can bring glory and honor to the Kingdom!

Remain in the Garden:

I've learned to remain in the garden through my submission to my husband in reverence for God. When my flesh tries to rebel against the plan of God, I renew my mind according to God's Word regardless of how I feel concerning a situation. Wives, we should be in continuous prayer for our headship. His sound mind is imperative for us and our next generation. Most importantly, I understand the extravagant wedding in the garden between my husband and me was a symbolic celebration of Christ receiving His church as His bride, fusing together to become one.

Wives if you are like me and you struggle with submission, say this prayer for a daily mind renewal:

"Our Father who art in heaven, hallowed would be Thy name; Thy kingdom come on earth as it is in heaven. I ask that you forgive me in the area of submission. Soften my heart to be the wife You created and purposed me to be. I thank You for equipping me as a wife to take on the spirit of a submissive wife as my husband continues to submit to You.

God, I simply thank You for my gift in the form of a husband. Help me to entrust the gift You have given to love me as You love Your church. Thank You for leaving Your Word behind to assist me as I take on the role as a wife and submit to the original plan of marriage.

I ask that You would reveal Your plans for our lives with clarity to my husband. Give me the words to assist him in

trusting You into our destiny in love. **Thank You in advance for enlarging our territory through our obedience and reverence towards You.** I thank You in advance because I know that this marriage will produce much fruit and that this marriage will be a pattern for kingdom marriages that will bring honor and glory to Your name. In Jesus name, amen.

Whenever my husband was given a prophetic word concerning me prior to our Courtship he was told, I was his Esther. I am learning to embrace the submissive spirit Esther walked in with humility and honor towards my King!

LaQuita Mason-Brown, is a native of Daingerfield, TX. She currently serves as an Active Duty Flight Medic in the United States Air Force. She has deployed in support of Operation Iraqi Freedom, Operation New Dawn, Operation Enduring Freedom, & Operation Inherent Resolve. She earned her Bachelors of Science Degree from Excelsior College. She will attend graduate school Spring 2016 at LSU. LaQuita, has a heart for the elderly population and plans to launch a Home Health Care Agency in the near future. She resides in Fayetteville, NC with her husband, Anqulais Brown. Her hobbies include traveling, working out, exploring new hiking trails, and experiencing exotic cuisines.

My Husband Was Never Meant to Be My God
Nephetina Serrano

Richard and I met when I was just a teenager in my last year of high school. I guess you could say he was my high school sweetheart, although we didn't go to school together. I worked while in school. One day while at my job, I was feeling lonely and sad. I went into the bathroom and prayed for God to send me a husband like my aunt's husband, who was so loving, caring, and affectionate towards her. I remember crying because I wanted a steady boyfriend and not just a fly-by-night relationship. Jesus heard my cry and answered that same day. Later that day, I met my husband. We were always very close and one another's best friends. Through the years, we have suffered loss in just about every way one could think of and we've weathered all types of storms that the devil has sent our way.

After 20 years in marriage, I found myself at a crossroads within my relationship with my husband, especially in how we were communicating. We had moved outside of our hometown for seven years, and although we were just two hours away, we rarely saw our family and friends. After the sudden death of my mother-in-law, we were faced with a decision of moving back home. During that time, my own mother needed to have surgery. Due the circumstances within our family, we felt it best to return home to be closer to our loved ones during this most difficult time of loss and devastation. At the time, I wanted to be near my mom after her surgery to assist her in recovery. Here we were moving back to our hometown and not very excited about it because we didn't foresee that as a desire or possibility within our future or at any point.

The devastation and sudden loss of my husband's mother was felt within his family and the community he grew up in, as most people in that area knew his mom. My own mother would need 3 to 6 months to heal after surgery with therapy and an in-home aide twice a week. Deciding to move back home after being away for seven years was neither an easy decision nor one that we were actually ready to endure.

Upon returning home, we realized it was the right decision for both of us. I was able to be there for my mom after surgery and my husband was able to be a present help and support for his family. That was certainly a relief for us, just to be able to be there for our families and not to have the stress of being too far away.

Time passed by so quickly and it wasn't long before we realized things were different here and that people had changed...or perhaps we were different. Although we were closer to our family and friends by location, we actually saw them less often than when we were a hundred miles away.

I must admit that being back in the city did provide some benefits. There were more job opportunities and I was able to take more on-campus classes at college. At some point, I noticed that things between my husband Richard and I were changing, and not in a good way. Things were spiraling downward quickly. We were literally on two ships passing by as I worked days and Richard worked nights. My schedule had grown very busy after returning to school and pursuing my ministry credentials to become an evangelist. I worked full-time, was enrolled in school as a part-time student, but sometimes also took 3-4 classes per semester and Saturday classes for ministry, not to mention having rotational duties at church.

In the beginning, after moving back home, I didn't realize there was a problem between Richard and I. I've learned along this journey that things can sometimes appear as though they're okay and just when I thought I was out of the storm, out of nowhere, the winds would begin to blow. Sometimes, although no rain is falling, your inner voice tells you to brace yourself because it's about to get rocky, but the Spirit tells you to stand still.

My husband and I have weathered many storms and suffered loss of many things. One thing we have always been able to do well is to communicate. We have always been there for one another. But this time, something was happening and I just couldn't figure out what. I was truly at a loss for what I should do in this situation. Here was my best friend and mate, the one I'd always been able to go to and we were not communicating as much. Due to our work situation, my schoolwork, and church responsibilities, we became very distant from each other. I noticed my husband becoming irritated easily and falling away from attending church service regularly, which told me that something was surely not right.

Due to my schedule with school, church, and work, I hadn't realized how distant we had become. During this time, we didn't live alone more than three months before we had a guests live with us. As we spent less time together, I realized that we were arguing more and more over any and everything. We didn't see eye-to-eye on many things. We began arguing daily, and before I knew it, a few months had gone by. I was feeling hurt and frustrated at this point. There was a time in our relationship when I had felt he was always there for me, but now, his actions had become cold and distant. I couldn't understand what was causing this behavior. We fussed about anything... school, the house, the car, our money, our church and our family.

This place in our relationship was a very challenging place for me as I began talk with the Lord. I prayed something like this: "Lord, I come before You asking for Your forgiveness and guidance concerning my role and responsibilities in keeping my husband happy. Lord, I desire to be a helpmeet to my husband, to build him up, not tear him down with my words or actions. I yield to You, my God, and I surrender my will to You, my Lord. Please help me to hear You when You speak. Father, touch my husband; heal his heart from hurt within the church. Help him, Lord, to put his trust only in You and not man or man's ability because man will fail him. Father, let him keep his eyes on the hills, looking to You alone because You are the author and the finisher of our faith. Help us, Lord, to stand united because we know, Father, that a house divided against itself cannot stand. We are weak. Make us strong. Where we have doubt, help our unbelief."

"I need you, Lord. We need you. I won't turn back now! Whatever change may be needed within me, Lord, please change me. I yield my vessel to You."

As the tears fell from my eyes, my heart burned, and I declared, "I will yet trust you, Lord." I believed God's heart is toward us and I was determined to wait on the Lord to change things within our marriage. It was at that moment that I began to speak to my situation and to the devil. I told the devil, "You are a liar and a defeated foe; my husband and I have victory, in Jesus name!"

My husband and I were always so close that we shared everything, did everything together, went everywhere together. We laughed, cried and supported each other through many of life's trials. And yet, there was a moment in time that was so unfamiliar to me. It was during this time that I realized a very key factor that would change the rest of my life.

During this moment I became aware that I had made my husband into my GOD. I realized that I depended on him more than I was dependent on God. I looked to him more than I looked to God. I realized now that I had to go through this process because had I not experienced this, I might not have been awakened by God. I had no idea I was putting my husband before my Lord and Savior.

Jesus is the giver of life and the One who died for my sins and your sins. Jesus clearly states in John 15:5-6 that "I am the vine; you are the branches. If a man remains in me and I in him, he will bear much fruit; apart from me you can do nothing. If anyone does not remain in me, he is like a branch that is thrown away and withers." God was not and will never be pleased when we put others before him.

The order of headship in my life was in the wrong order and as Deuteronomy 6-5 says, "Love the Lord your God with all your heart and with all your soul and with all your strength."

The enemy will use whatever ammunition we give him against us. He'll make you think that your marriage was a mistake. He'll make you feel like your husband just doesn't understand you. He'll try to convince you to take a break, that your husband doesn't love you or that you're not going to make it like this, etc. We, as wives, must always remember to PRAY. These are tactics to separate you.

I began to pray and to ask God to change me, my heart, my tolerance, and my understanding; I began to focus on God and not my situation. I prayed to the Lord, "Hear my heart, oh Lord. My eyes are ever toward Thee. Lord, I need You to speak to my heart that I may hear from You. Lord, I desire to be used by You, to be pleasing to You. Show me how to love, Lord, and how to respect and honor my husband. I will look toward the hills from where cometh my help. I thank You, God, for being my King of Kings, the lifter up of my head, my joy, my hope, my all in all."

Wives, I began to realize that change needed to begin with me. My marriage has been and still is a journey in progress toward oneness. I'm learning to trust only in God, who will never fail me, and to not put unrealistic expectations on my husband. I'm looking only to Christ to fulfill His purpose in my life. Today, I look to God for everything and trust man for nothing. When the enemy attempts to bring the wrong thoughts my way, I'll cancel those thoughts with God's Word. Philippians 4:8 says, "Finally, brothers and sisters, whatever is true, whatever is noble, whatever is right, whatever is pure, whatever is lovely, whatever is admirable—if anything is excellent or praiseworthy—think about such things."

God desires for us to walk in harmony and oneness within our marriage and to have a good success in it so that we can bear fruit and be living examples to what God can and will do in our marriage.

In time, I witnessed God turning my situation around. Without my interference, God began to change my husband's heart. We had a long conversation about what we each desired and how we could work on making those things happen. He returned to service. Going regularly, he took a stance that he would not be moved by man and that he'd walk the path God laid out for him. He made a vow to God that he would not give up. We were referred to a wonderful biblical counselor, who we keep in contact with even now.

The Word of God says, "Where no counsel *is*, the people fall: but in the multitude of counselors, *there is* safety." ***Proverbs 11:14***

Today, Richard and I are continuing on this journey toward oneness, working in ministry together and keeping God in the center of our marriage. Knowing that we are better together and having the power of two in agreement is a mighty force. Remember, a covenant is not a contract to be broken; it is a vow to God first and then to one another.

As a life coach, marriage counselor, inspirational empowerment speaker, visionary, and advisor/mentor, this evangelist, along with her husband, is on a quest to rebuild the family one marriage at a time. Evangelist Serrano and her husband, Richard, founded Covenant Marriages, Inc., where they are mentoring and coaching couples in crisis. The Serranos are reaching beyond the walls, helping couples who are in transitional phases within their marriage and life, seeking to restore the family through biblical counseling.

Evangelist Serrano is the Executive Vice President and co-founder of Philadelphia Covenant Rescue for Marriages, a non-profit organization that is designed to help married couples and families in crisis who are in urgent need of support during turbulent times within their marriage by providing 24-hour assistance.

Serrano received Christ at the early age of 12 and began walking in her calling at age 19. She attends Mt. Airy Church of God In Christ in Philadelphia, P.A., where she has been a member for over 25 years and serves on the local and jurisdictional level. Her love for people fuels her mission to encourage, uplift, and inspire couples to journey into their individual God-given purpose and destiny while achieving the ultimate goal, "oneness" within their marriage.

You can hear Evangelist Serrano and her husband every third Thursday on the "We Are One" Empowerment International Conference call. She counts it a privilege to serve God's people and a blessing to be called servant. To God be the Glory!

*In Sickness
And
In Health*

A Word From
Eraina Tinnin

When asked to write a foreword for Wives on Fire, I felt it an honor and a privilege. I have been married for 22 years. My husband and I were together 2 years prior to marriage. If there is anyone reading this book that has been married longer than a day, you know that marriage is work. There will be good days, bad days, happy days, and sad days. Through it all you are to be united as one. When two people from different backgrounds and life experiences try to come together as one, it is not an easy task. In addition to the differences, life also happens; married couples experience job loss, death of a loved one, illness, financial woes, and much more. The stories in this book will enable wives to see that they are NOT alone. *Wives on Fire* will share the testimonies of 32 wives and how God saw them through. No matter what obstacle came their way they all have one thing in common; they made it through and are STILL together.

Eraina Tinnin is a speaker, affectionately called an inspirational powerhouse, professional marriage coach and entrepreneur. She has been named an "Encourager" because of her unfailing ability to lift the spirits of others. She is an inspirational and relationship staff writer with Simply Elevate Magazine, author of Becoming a Beautiful You and program co-host with Forever Sisters Radio Broadcast. She has a Master's Degree in Human Services with a specialization in Marriage & Family Therapy from Liberty University. She is a wife, mother and ministry leader. You may visit her website at www.erainatinninonline.com.

A Word From
Dr. Chevelta A. Smith

Pain. Struggle. Disappointment. Who would have ever thought that marriages, including Christian marriages, would be challenged with such circumstances? More importantly, for those who do experience such events, there is often no one they can confide in for help. As a result, they suffer in silence—alone. *Wives on Fire* is a book which introduces you to the dynamic stories of many different Christian women who reveal their tremendous personal challenges within their marital journey. Addictions, extra marital affairs, and so on, are transparently shared with such amazing authenticity.

The complication of stories within *Wives on Fire* serves as a guide to assist women, of all walks of life, in learning how to navigate through the various challenges of marriage, without giving up. As a marriage ministry leader and teacher for over 15 years, I understand all too well, the need for such a tool to assist women in triumphing over the obstacles that can often be presented in marriage. Furthermore, as a marriage conference speaker, I have personally seen the deep seeded heart and resentment many women experience as a direct result of these obstacles. This book serves as a roadmap to marital victory, as women learn how to overcome the tests they can be faced with themselves and with their partners.

Dr. Chevelta A Smith,

Board Certified Obstetrician/Gynecologists, Founder of B.E.D. Marriage Movement and Raw Medicine; Published Author, Can I Push? Understanding the Process to Delivering Your Purpose.

Seek Counsel
Carrie Clark

I was in love and you couldn't tell me otherwise! I fell madly in love with what I hoped to be my soul mate. We both were in love and, for the first time for me, it was amazing. I called it a breath of fresh air. He was my best friend in the world. We weren't perfect, just the perfect team. One day I was in the kitchen cooking dinner and the day was going by so slow. I heard him come in the house. He was on the phone and was excited while talking to one of his friends. He asked me, if he asked me to marry him would I turn him down? I said, "What, crazy?" His response was, as he gets down on one knee, "Carrie will you marry me?" I had the biggest smile on my face! First before I answered I said, "Stop playing!" We laughed, and he said "I'm serious!" We went back and forth because I was in shock! I knew I was capable of being a wife but I didn't think he was ready. I hugged and kissed him and couldn't wait to tell my family. I was so excited that night I kept asking him was he serious. I said, "Are we really getting married?" He said, "Yes, Babe, we are getting married." The next day, I texted and called the people that loved and supported us. Everyone I told at that moment was ecstatic and happy for us. My mother was so excited for us. She just kept saying, "Awwwww!" Every time she said it I got goosebumps!

Months had gone by and my God mother and I went out for the day. She asked me if we were going to get pre-marital counseling. Big question! Good question! I told her I had to talk to him and see what he wanted to do. The Lord was not the head of our relationship and my personal relationship with the Lord was not where it should've been. I regret it today because I believe things would've been extremely different had we made the Lord the head. If things were right it wouldn't have gone left. By this time everyone knew we were engaged and we had picked the place where we wanted to have the wedding and the reception. My parents gave us a huge engagement party and we had so much fun. It was so amazing to see everyone who loved us and supported us. He had family come from out of town to support as well. That made him way more comfortable than I expected. It was just beautiful.

At that point I knew my wedding was going to be so beautiful. I even got emotional about it. We danced and took so many pictures just having so much fun. Now, I must explain that he was more on the anti-social side and I am the total opposite. I think that's what made it so interesting because after being in a relationship with him it calmed me down a bit and I became more patient and always was on "chill mode". I was the party and he was the home body, so he usually stayed home during a lot of events. I just got used to it. I didn't like it but I loved him so I just didn't make a big deal about it. Some things he attended so I'll give him credit for that. At the engagement party he was having so much fun with everyone. Everyone loved him as well as us together. During the next month or so we went to a couple of food tastings for the reception and finally picked a place. My parents offered to pay for the reception as a gift to us. His mother also gifted us money for the reception. When my parents told us about their gift to us we were excited. We made our guest list to include both sides of our families and our friends. We started with 175 and we were able to get it down to 130. I never had the chance to ask him about counseling, or I knew what his answer would be, so I just acted like I forgot about it. Honestly in my heart I knew he wasn't really going to agree to let "someone come in and tell us how to run our relationship". A part of me wanted to ask him and the other part was like girrrrlllll you know how private he is. But I knew pre-marital counseling was helpful and such a blessing, I just had to convince him. In my mind I kept saying he would do it! We had been through so much at that point, I figured the only thing counseling could do was help. Sometimes as women we tend to go to church build our relationship with the Lord in the hopes that our man follows us. I wasn't thinking like that at the time and I should have been because I knew better and he knew the Lord for himself. I should've been in ministry and showing my family that the Lord is the head of our family. But I wasn't involved in ministry at that time so asking him about counseling was much harder. I regret not building the most important relationship.

At this time my dresses for my bridesmaids were picked out. This process was so much fun. Having support from our parents made the process less stressful. We looked in magazines for tuxedos for his guys and he was into it, which made me more excited. I decided to call my bridesmaids to go the bridal store to try the dresses on. I even picked out my dress. It was so beautiful that when I tried it on I sat in the dressing room for a few minutes and cried because I was so happy. In that moment I realized how beautiful I'd become. It was something about being in that dress and I knew if he saw me it would be a breath of fresh air! My girls tried on their dresses and made their first payments.

One day while driving he and I had a little time to ourselves and I said babe how do you feel about pre-marital counseling? He was silent for a few moments and I repeated myself. He shrugged and said, "I don't!" I asked him, "What do you mean you don't know?!" He said, "I don't think about it." I said, But you should at least consider it." He said, "I don't need counseling. I love you and you love me. We don't need anyone telling us how to do that." Needless to say we didn't agree on pre-marital counseling. I also didn't want it to turn into an argument. Time went on and things were happening that we needed so much help with. We were breaking up and getting back together, our communication began to be horrible, which lead to us being disrespectful toward each other. We started arguing more and the distance began. I didn't want to be bothered and he felt the same. He would come and I would go and I would come and he would go. The stability took a turn for the worse and things changed drastically. The trust was gone due to certain behaviors from the both of us. I stopped trusting him and he stopped trusting me. After all of that we were not making it. The wedding was called off and we broke up but still lived together. It was so hurtful because, again, this was my first true love–my first time actually being in love with someone I thought I'd spend the rest of my life with. I felt like he took the easy way out and caused so much pain. I still fought but he didn't. I had never had these feelings about anyone.

The happiness had gone, too, and there wasn't anything left. The more I fought the more he pulled away. On my last day of school, which was another milestone and very important to me, he came to me and said he wasn't happy and I asked why? He kind of danced around it and blamed it on the finances but he was "happy" elsewhere. I didn't take that route because I figured if we fixed it before we can do it again. Yet he did go there and I was so hurt at that point. I packed all of his things and told his friends to come and get them. I was filled with hurt, anger, and rage. We had one car and he had it doing God knows what and not taking my calls, so that was it for me. My heart was truly broken for the first time ever.

I picked up my phone and called an old friend. I shouldn't have done it but I did and we talked that whole night. He said everything I needed to hear. Just from that one conversation I learned so much. By the time my ex-fiancé came home, I felt empty. I was so numb I didn't even pray! I was truly embarrassed because people would tell me things he was doing. He was truly all about himself. I never concerned myself with what people would say about us being apart. Everything we had was gone. From the time of the break up there was so much going on it was unbelievable. I was scorned and still filled with that pain and anger. Every action had a reaction so I started hurting him. I didn't do so much of the things he had done but I caused my fair share of pain toward him.

My children were hurt behind what happened. It was just so hard. We also suffered the loss of a child. We both had to watch our son take his last breath and that broke our hearts even more. My pregnancy was so stressful and we were fighting more than ever. On Halloween of that year I thought I was having Braxton Hicks and they were painful, I went home and got some rest. He came that next day to check on us and then left. At this point, I was extremely stressed but it was more to it than that! A few days later we went to the doctor together and heard awful news. The doctor told me I would have to have an emergency C-section. That was so hard. In my heart I blamed him, which made me blame myself because I should've just taken care of myself. I had the support of a really great friend! A couple of days later I gave birth to a handsome little boy named Kristian, who was so little and cute. I saw happiness again in my ex's eyes and that was the last time I saw that look! The doctor told us my Kristian had Hydrops (A serious condition that occurs when abnormal amounts of fluid buildup in two or more body areas of a fetus or newborn)! I knew one thing; I believed my son would make it through! A few hours later the doctor came in my room with terrible news. He said they revived my son 4 times already and it was becoming more and more difficult and painful for him and he was only 2 lbs. I cried so much in those few minutes! I was extremely hurt! We went to the NICU and sat with him. The pastor baptized him and all I could do was cry. The doctor said they couldn't revive him anymore because it would cause permanent brain damage, so his dad and I had to make a choice we didn't ever want to make. As I watched him squeeze his dad's finger I felt so empty inside. He looked at me and I cried harder. The nurse let me hold him and a few minutes later we heard the long loud beep and we watched him take his last breath. The absolute worst moment in my entire life! I just kissed him and hugged him and his father hugged me and I hugged him back. We both just cried and, for the most part, he was very supportive. We had each other to lean on in those moments. Only we could understand it. I didn't want to let my son go so we kept him in the room with us. Everyone was so loving, supportive, and helpful, especially the hospital staff. They offered us a photo shoot so we could have memories of Kristian. My life was never the same. It was even more painful. We had a service for him. My amazing Godparents came and did his service. Family came and supported us, so we were surrounded by love. I just wanted my child back. I had to explain to my other children that their brother passed away. It was so hard and I still don't know how I got through it all!

It was Gods twins, grace and mercy, that delivered me from so much pain. You don't know your strength unless it's all you have left. What was even worse is when I went back for my check up, my doctor told me that my son saved my life! Going through all the tests and results, had I not made it to the doctor that day we both would've passed by my due date. It hurts to know that someone so innocent can save your life and theirs doesn't even really begin. I would never want to be in the predicament where my children have to give up their lives to save mine; I'd give them mine in a heartbeat!! I pride myself on being a great mother. But to know that this sacrifice was made is still hurtful in many ways, I am grateful and there isn't really much to say but I wish he was here with all of us. I'll always remember what my son did for me and his sisters and brothers. The most difficult painful thing I've ever had to go through. One thing I know is I never question God! I just prayed for clarity, joy, some sort of peace, and love! Everything was just a domino effect! There wasn't anything left in that relationship with my ex. We loved each other still yet had absolutely no way of showing it. We have an incredible bond that neither of us will ever share with anyone else.

As a child I was taught that love was an action word, meaning if you love me show me. So showing love went in its own direction as well. I blamed him for so much. I believed if he hadn't ruined our family, Kristian would've been living but I had no control over that and it just became unbearable to even try to communicate with him.. Every time we talked we had so much negative to say about the other. I brought up his infidelity and lies and it became such a negative and dark place! We both were in a dark place. Some place neither of us expected to be. It hurt the both of us because deep down we believed in the potential of our relationship. We both used excuses and a bunch of things just to not be hurt but we both were hurt.

A week after my son passed away I started praying, going to church, and mending my relationship with God! I prayed more and asked less. I tried to understand everything that had happened within those years. I was so broken hearted and I couldn't believe it. After separating and mending my relationship, I began to understand so much. The one thing I now understand after having my heart broken is that help was needed and we didn't try. I had to face that. I didn't try!!!!! We needed counseling badly and had we put our pride aside, as a union, and asked for help, we probably would be in a blessed and prosperous union right now! We could both be happy elsewhere but we will always wonder and wish things could be different. I started to have a small place in my heart where hate developed for him, mainly because I looked to him as the leader and I let him lead and it wasn't where we were supposed to be. I just really wish we had gone to pre-marital counseling! We talk and say what we wished we wouldn't have done but what does that solve? It's just confirmation that we both are still hurting. I was afraid to ask the Lord what He wants from me and him. I pray for the both of us all the time. We are in two different places but hurt has changed us, pain has affected us in so many ways. I still love him so much and I know he loves me the same. That will never change. He reassures me of that all the time, even now. The love is and will always be there. As much as I told myself he can't possibly love me and do the things that he did yet I know the feeling. If the Lord wants us together again He will make that happen.

The lesson in it all is if you need help get it! If your church has resources that help, don't be prideful. Being prideful made me lose so much. Get all the help you can get! If you don't seek counsel things will happen and you won't be able to handle it. Without the Lord being the head, and seeking counsel, everything else will fall out of place. It's a shame because I can only imagine how blessed we'd be if we would've put the Lord first, communicated better, and sought counsel.

Today I encourage everyone to work on building a relationship with the Lord and He will provide all of your needs. In all thy ways acknowledge HIM!

Carrie Clark is an amazing mother of 4 beautiful children and an angel. She is a woman of many talents but the talent that's most appealing is her writing. Writing stories at the tender age of 9 years old, she's been writing movie scripts and short stories for years and is passionate about her work. A hard working, educated, as well as, a dedicated woman; she's been to her lowest and now wants to reach her highest. She loves the Lord and will happily tell her testimony and where the Lord has brought her from for the benefit of others. She's grown into a beautiful woman who knows her worth and what's worth working hard for. The love she has for her children is such a beautiful blessing and all she wants to do is make them proud while her angel watches and protects.

Faith To Conceive
Crystal Peurifoy

It is often while we're in the midst of life's most tumultuous storms that God calls us to be the most calm and faith-filled. By trusting that God will never give us more than we can handle; and that He will steadfastly remain that beacon of light, faith, and hope through all the chaos, confusion, and questioning that tries to take over our inner silence and serenity, we'll be able to see His gifts and His blessings in *every* moment of *every* day, even when stepping into an elevator or when crying out alone into the darkness of the night.

While I know I am blessed not only to be married to the love of my life, Henry A Peurifoy, Jr (aka: my Boaz), but also to be able to continue to enjoy and embrace so many countless and wondrous moments with him; there have been some very challenging, stress-filled, and not-so-great times during this 11+ year marriage, even with all the endless love and respect we have for each other. Undoubtedly the biggest hurdles, tests of our faith, and heartaches have stemmed from trying to conceive a baby and the birth of our beautiful daughter, appropriately named, Faith.

During the very first year of our marriage, my husband and I were delighted to discover I was pregnant. You couldn't harness our excitement; we were so delighted and joyful that we were starting our family. On my first appointment to have my first ultrasound; however, the baby had no heartbeat. Upon receiving the news that we miscarried what was to be our first child, we headed out from that appointment feeling devastated. When we stepped into the elevator in the hospital that day, in disbelief, sadness, and confusion, we saw a woman in the elevator crying inconsolably. Without hesitation, we asked her what was wrong. She shared with us that her house had burned to the ground. In that moment, we prayed with her right there in the elevator in spite of our own current personal struggle.

Within just moments of receiving the news that we had miscarried, God showed us that life, love, and hope are not *only* about what we were going through, in the midst of our own personal trials, but about instinctively and faithfully knowing when to witness and help others in the midst of theirs. Being of service to this lady that we didn't know changed the atmosphere for us for the rest of that day.

2 Timothy 4:2 states, "Preach the word, be prepared in season and out of season rebuke and encourage with great patience and careful instruction."

Early the next morning, I awoke with anxiety knowing that I was still carrying our baby in my body and had to wait 7 days to go to the operating room for the scheduled surgery. Every morning leading up to the surgery I awoke with a different emotion remembering all the miracles Jesus had done. I told Henry if JESUS raised Lazarus from the dead surely if He wanted to He could start the heart beat in our child. At that point Henry wasn't sure if he had married a crazy Lady or if my faith was that strong.

The baby's heart beat never returned. After the longest week of my life, we went to the operating room and had the Dilation and Evacuation completed.

I'm sharing this intimate part of my life to help any sisters who are dealing with infertility, and isolation.

A few months later I became pregnant again and was so excited until 6 weeks into the pregnancy when I started bleeding.

I went to the hospital and was told by the doctor that he didn't think the baby was going to make it and I was losing a lot of blood. With that news my husband starting praying and told me to have faith and that we would have this baby. After lying in the hospital for one month I was told I could go home and needed to stay on bed rest until I delivered my baby.

Now there I was going from just getting married and working for the last 20 years, to going out, on what I thought at that time was going to be a horrible time alone, while Henry was at work. Little did I know JESUS was sitting me down in preparation for a double blessing. Not only was I going to get my little girl that I had been praying for the last 20 years, but he was also going to minister to me on a personal level without any distractions.

I looked up and the closest person to me was in another state and they couldn't get to me. I cried out to the Lord asking, why was He leaving me in this very uncomfortable place?

In Mark 6:31, Jesus said lets go off by ourselves to a quiet place and rest awhile. He said this because there were so many people coming and going that JESUS and his apostles didn't even have time to eat. Do you know that when there are many distractions around us we can't hear clearly from the Lord?

During the next 6 months there was a lot more episodes of bleeding and back and forth to the hospital. Henry, who was new to married life, had to cook, clean, and take care of me. So I continued to cry out to the Lord asking Him why was I being a burden to my husband when I was supposed to be his helpmate. I was reminded of Gen 2:18 (NLT) where the Lord GOD said, "It is not good for the man to be alone. I will make a helper who is just right for him."

We may not always fit the traditional role as a wife by cooking and cleaning. But God will have us to be the right fit for

147

our husband by praying and encouraging them even from our place of being still. Now there we were newlyweds with restrictions on being intimate with each other. The tension was high, even though it was only for a season. When GOD is in the midst of blessing you with a miracle, there are minor issues going on around you that will distract you from the major blessing coming your way. Please don't major in the minors.

Henry and I were forced to be still and depend on GOD. We had no control over life and could only pray daily that we would have a healthy baby girl. Daily I heard this still, quiet voice saying continue to trust me, stay faithful with your devotion, and pray continually.

During our difficult time I often wondered how the Lord would bring us out of this storm. After 9 months and 1 week Faith was born healthy. Yes, she was a week late on the doctor's schedule, but it was her appointed time that God had ordained for her life.

Henry and I are so grateful for our Miracle Blessing Daughter, Faith

The lesson in all this is we have to always listen to that still, small voice. When interruptions happen during your marriage (and they will happen), we must stop and be still and put on the whole armor of God.

Ephesians 6:10-12 states, "Be strong in the Lord and in his mighty power. Put on all of God's armor so that you will be able to stand firm against all strategies of the devil. For we are not fighting against flesh and blood enemies but against evil rulers and authorities of the unseen world; against mighty powers in this dark world, and against evil spirits in the heavenly places."

For those struggling with infertility, miscarriages, or other difficulties of pregnancy, I know what you're going through and I have compassion for you. While knowing that others understand might help ease your pain temporarily, there is someone whose compassion and love for you and your husband can comfort you even more–God! Romans 5:8 tells us, *"But God demonstrates his own love for us, in that while we were still sinners, Christ died for us."* God sent His *only* Son to die for *our* sins! As women desiring our own child, we of all people can certainly understand how profoundly difficult it would be to allow our child to die for someone else. God loves us *that* much; He longs for a relationship with each of us, and He wants to bless us. During each of our lives there are things that will be challenging, even times when we will be brought to our knees in sorrow, pain, or grief, but we must remember that God is there for us, ALWAYS. All we need to do is to call out to Him. Sometimes, probably most of the time, we are focusing too much on our own lives, our own situations, and we don't take the time to pray and ask God for help and guidance. Proverbs 3:5 says, *"Trust in the Lord with all your heart, and do not rely on your own understanding."* That says to me that although I may not understand God's plans or His timing, or I don't understand why I am not holding a child in my arms right at this very moment even though I so desperately long to, I need to trust in the Lord. In my mind, trust and faith go hand-in-hand. Scripture tells us, *"Faith is the confidence that what we hope for will actually happen; it gives us assurance about things we cannot see."* - Hebrews 11:1. Faith, confidence, trust; these are all things I need to focus on more while focusing less on my troubles and tribulations. We live in a fallen world where there is evil, sin, and where bad things do happen. God doesn't make these things happen; instead, He uses these situations to make good things happen. Losing a child is devastating whether it is born or unborn. God wants to use your situation and turn it into good; draw near to Him and behold His blessings.

149

I would compare myself to Sarah in the Bible she was 90 years old when she conceived I was 40 and our generation now 40 is the 90 on having children. Be Blessed!

Crystal Peurifoy has been married to her wonderful husband, Henry, for more than 10 years, is the proud mother of two children, and the proud grandmother of one granddaughter. She's been a member of Sharon Baptist Church for more than 25 years where she serves as a Deaconess and held positions as a Confirmation Counselor and Usher for many years.

Crystal is the Owner and CEO of HCP Healthcare, and a Medical Billing & Coding Consultant/Instructor, with more than 25 years' experience in Healthcare operations. She has extensive knowledge in ICD-9, ICD-10, CPT, HCPCS, DRG and APC. She also has experience across varied healthcare settings including short term acute care hospitals, long term acute care facilities, critical access hospitals, and physician practice settings; auditing service company consultant (RAC), HIM consultant, instructor for ICD-9-CM diagnosis and procedural coding; CPT-4 procedure and professional fee E&M coding, and medical terminology, anatomy and physiology. She has a high degree of professional integrity and dedication, organizational skills, independence, and motivation.

150

Thriving Through the Grace of God
Elizabeth Banks

It was a cold Saturday in December. I was working a full-time job, a part-time job and also attending school full-time. After taking my seven-year-old son Taj clothes shopping, to the movies, then to Toys R Us to get him something he wanted to compensate the feeling of neglect I had due to my busy schedule, I was literally beat. However, he wanted to go to the car wash which was directly across the street. I said no but he was persistent so he won me over. While the car was going through (he stayed in, I got out because car washes frighten me) there stood a tall handsome guy staring at me who looked as if he had just finished work. He noticed my glance and asked if I frequented the car wash because he never had seen me here before. My response was "No, this is my first time here and that I was only here because of my son." He then said "He would have to thank my son in the future for bringing him his wife." We had small talk which seemed as if we'd known each other for years. The chemistry was unbelievable so we exchanged numbers.

While getting to know one another I shared with him that I was from a broken home, my mother was an addict, my sister and my relationship was strange, and that my last relationship was abusive. Also that I was not looking for anything serious. He shared with me that his mother was legally blind, his father passed when he was four, he was the eldest of four, he was once married, and had five children with his wife who had passed away ten years prior from. He expressed how his children were taken from him and all the things that he has gone through trying

151

to get them back. I know a lot of women would have run. I even had conversations with the elders of my family and they pretty much told me to run. But there was something about him that drew me to him. Aside from his good looks, there were his ambitions and his strength. Our talks were deep rooted and penetrating. He made love to my mind, he made me feel as if I was the only woman in the world, and he was the lighter to my cigarette, the sugar to my tea. When I heard his name I would light up like a Christmas tree; when I saw his face my insides would melt. He took care of me, of us AND he loved my son like the father Taj never had. We just connected on so many levels until it became scary. So I started to second guess myself and I stepped back from the relationship. To my surprise he understood and gave me my space. (Another turn ON!!) I prayed to God to give me a sign. I can't say for certain what the sign was, but I said yes to continue moving forward with the relationship.

We moved into a larger house while fighting to get his children back. Blending two families was a challenge. Dealing with three teenage girls with different personalities, attitudes and the lack of motherly love and affection took a toll. Not that I didn't want to give it because nurturing flows natural with me, but they just weren't receptive to what I was offering. The oldest child, a son didn't stay but the youngest child, a boy who was the same age as my son was torn between what was being fed to him by the sisters and what his dad and I were trying to instill in him. My son finally had a playmate (and so what I thought) was adapting well. But that wouldn't last. The children didn't want to stay. To me they were used to living one way then having to move in with their dad and fiancé and child, experiencing a different set of rules and structure and they didn't want to get down with the program.

Between the tug-of-wars of the children four years into the relationship we had a child together. He was born when I was just twenty-four weeks pregnant. He spent the first 8 months of his life in the hospital. There were so many obstacles he overcame. We couldn't hold him for the first 3 months. He experienced everything from breathing tubes to blood infections, heart murmuring, and two blood clots on his heart, a ruptured intestine, and veins collapsing so they had to put the IV in his head. He overcame it all. They said he would need eye surgery but God prevailed. They said he would need heart surgery, but God prevailed. They said he would have learning disabilities because of the heavy oxygen and delayed fine motor skills; he wouldn't be able to keep up with other children his age physically because of muscle spasms. With a little physical and occupational therapy he surpassed every test every time he had an appointment to the point they discharged him early from his development case study. At age six today, he is the smartest, brightest soldier and has not skipped a beat. Again, God has prevailed.

In February, a month before our youngest son's second birthday and a month before my oldest son's fourteenth birthday we married. That August I found out I was carrying our second child, a girl, who came in April. For her first birthday it was going to be something special. As residents of Philly and in search of her perfect outfit, we felt led to Atlantic City, NJ. On this particular day the children had doctor's appointments, so it was my intention for them to go with us. But my husband said that we should take them to school so we could be in and out. So I agreed. We dropped them off at school and headed across the Ben Franklin. About twenty minutes after crossing the bridge, I reclined my seat and fell asleep. I awoke to the truck riding over the ridges on the side of the road on route 42. The next thing I felt, I was lifted out of my seat and felt as if I were in a pinball machine. The truck rolled over at least five times off the embankment. The only thing I could think of was "LORD, please forgive my soul; when this truck comes to a stop I know I will be dead". The truck stopped. I heard my husband screaming my name, I heard people coming towards us but I couldn't respond. I think I was in a state of shock. His screams turned into cries and pleas for me not to be dead. I opened my eyes and tried to move but quickly realized that I was pinned between the roof and the dashboard and it was upside down. I finally let out a loud scream and heard my husband praise and thank the Lord. I did not have on my seat belt, but my husband did. Once rescue got there it was easier for them to get him out; they just had to cut his seat belt. I had to wait for what they call "the jaws of life" to get me out. The rescue gave me oxygen since I was hyperventilating, because I didn't think I would see my husband and children again. If the dashboard would have stopped two centimeters more, my arm and head would have been crushed. When the jaws of life finally got there I heard them say to cut the power because I was lying on the inside of the roof and the light was burning my side. When they attached and cranked then pulled, I heard all of the metal in my ear. They stopped and the car went back on top of my head. I heard concern in their voices of the truck possibly sliding and or catching fire. My adrenaline spiked along with my pressure and I smacked the lady with my free right hand because she would not pull me out. They tried it again on the count of three. Simultaneously they lifted the car and pulled me out. I believe that was the most grateful moment in my life. We were air vacced to Atlantic City memorial hospital. My husband was discharged a day later with absolutely nothing wrong with him. I was discharged two days later with minor burns and scratches to my back and a lot of soreness. Yes, that is all. While waiting on rescue, there was a lady that stayed with me, held my hand, prayed with me and rejoiced with me. She said she was looking at a vehicle where there should have been no survivors. I learned later that my husband was trapped for an hour and a half and I was trapped for over two hours. Once again the God I serve is a mighty awesome God. There are no words I can form to express my gratefulness. Once again He prevailed.

The following year my husband became very ill because of complications with diabetes. It was the worst I have seen. He had rapid weight loss, real bad neuropathy in his feet, was on five different medications a day, and infection after infection, hospital stays after hospital stays; they sent him home several times with a pic line (an IV line that goes to the heart). I had to keep that area as clean as possible to prevent an infection to his heart all while working, helping with homework, shopping, cooking, cleaning and maintaining the house and bills because he was unable to work. This lasted approx. 4-5 years. This impacted him to the core of his being. He was in a state where he felt man-less, and worthless; he was unable to take care of his family as he once did and the entire burden was left on me. Of course it took a strong toll on me. My oldest son picked up a lot of responsibility. It was a time where I thought I was ready to surrender. I tried my best to keep it together as a wife, a mother, a worker, and all the many other hats that we wear. It wore on my body, my strength. But no one noticed the internal pain and struggle I was going through. I always kept a smile on my face because of the God that I serve. I believed that there was a purpose for everything.

Today I say that my marriage is thriving only through the grace of God. We are not where we should and want to be but we are definitely not where we were. We are growing in self and in the Lord. My mother is now a recovering addict; all praise be to the Lord. The oldest son and the five children are currently living on their own. There is a four-year-old daughter and six-year-old son who keep us both on our toes.

Let us pray: God I thank you for your mercy, all of our children, for guidance and protection, and to be covered in the Lord's blood. Father God I pray that the bloodshed of our Christ Jesus will not be in vain and that we will be obedient to your will. May you receive the increase in our marriage so that it will be a reflection of the union and what you put together that we will be a blessing to those who are struggling in marriage. I pray for continual growth and change that you may get the increase in Christ Jesus name we pray amen.

Biblical wife comparison: I would like to say I can relate myself with Sarah, Abraham's wife. Her principles of submissiveness to her husband and faith are that God is working through her husband to accomplish what is best for her and her family.

Having Faith
Fern Chandler

I moved to Delaware in 2001 because I heard the Lord tell me to stay under my pastor, who had relocated to Delaware to lead a church there. Even after moving, I still worked in Conshohocken, P.A., which was about a 45-minute commute each way. I desired to work closer to home.

It was just another Sunday when my phone rang, and on the other side was Aunt D informing me of a job opportunity that sounded too good to be true. I called; the voice that answered was deep and friendly. "How can I help you?" he said. I answered, "You can help me get a job."

Once he learned that I wasn't computer-savvy, he helped me complete the application over the phone. He needed my resume, so we met at church. I learned that Darin worked in the church security ministry and was a leader in the men's ministry. I recall even calling my Bishop and asking about Darin; his answer was, "He's a good guy."

We talked a few times afterwards, but I couldn't help but wonder where all of these conversations were going. So being Holy Ghost-bold, I asked "Why are you still calling me? I'm not looking for a boyfriend." To my surprise, he answered, "Good. I'm not looking for a girlfriend. I'm looking for a wife."

Running scared, I did what comes naturally to me and hung up the phone without even saying goodbye. I recall calling my family and telling them that he was not my type. The response that I got would change the way I saw him: "What is your type? And I thought you were giving up on your type?"

You guessed it…after much prayer, fasting, and even facing my personal fears about making the wrong decisions, as I had done before, I decided to trust God. When he called, once I was clear God was giving me the okay, I said yes to the new possibility of being a wife.

We began to court, planning our wedding over the course of a year. I had always dreamed of a Princess Diana wedding, including a tiara, extra-long train, eight groomsmen and bridesmaids, three flower girls, bell chimers, a gift-bearer, a horse and buggy, a stretch limo, and a large reception, all topped off with a two week honeymoon, one on land and one on sea. Can you imagine the cost? The wedding day went as I had dreamed and the costs were beyond our wildest dreams. We are still paying 15 years later.

I expected my husband to be my knight in shining armor. I expected him to:

1. Pay ALL bills I ever had,
2. To have all the answers to all of my dilemmas,
3. To talk to me and to share his dreams,
4. To fit into my family,
5. And to want to have children immediately.

However, not one of these things occurred when I expected them to, how I expected them to, or the way I expected them to happen. My reality was so far from my expectations.

1. All my bills did NOT get paid;
2. I still have dilemmas without answers;
3. We barely talked at all, and he dreamed about playing his Xbox;
4. Family had to fit into 45-minute visits;
5. No more than a year later, I experienced my first miscarriage, followed by two more after that.

One morning after the fourth, I remember turning to Darin, asking, "If we were to have a daughter, what would we name her?" In a deep, strong, secure voice, he said, "Faith. It's going to take faith to get her here."

Hebrews 11:1: "Now faith is the substance of things hoped for, the evidence of things not seen." Hebrews 11:6: "But without faith, it is impossible to please him, for he that cometh to God must believe that he is, and that he is a rewarder of them that diligently seek him." He hung these Scriptures over my mirror, where they could be seen every day.

In spite of the Scriptures, I impatiently decided that it was time to see a specialist. We sat down with the specialist, and after many tests, he let us know that the blood that would be used to feed my child was too thick and not getting to the child. I remember him saying, "I can fix this. I can take from your husband and take from you and I can get you pregnant." He repeated this three times, and on the third time, Darin had had enough. He stated, "Only God himself can do that."

While leaving the doctor's office, he spoke out and said, "Of course, you could always just take one aspirin a day!" At that very moment, I heard the Lord say to me, "That's it…one aspirin a day and wait on me." Month after month, aspirin after aspirin for five years, my faith was challenged. I was living out Mark 9:24, which says, "Lord, I believe: help thou mine unbelief." The specialist said, "Not yet;" my body said, "Not yet;" but my husband never said, "Not yet." I remember crying out to God in despair and finally submitting to His will being done. At that time I allowed myself to enjoy my husband, my stepdaughter, and the life we had together.

In 2009, I found myself much like Sarah, Abraham's wife, while in front of my OB-GYN, laughing and saying, "Shall I bear a child? I am 43 years old." At the time appointed, according to the time of life, Faith A. Chandler was born. Today, she is a free-spirited, joy-filled 5–year-old. Every time I look at the face of my daughter, I am reminded that according to Jeremiah 29:11, "I know the thoughts that I think toward you, says the Lord, thoughts of peace, and not of evil, to give you an expected end." God has a plan with an expected end for Faith and for all of you.

So here is the question I have for many of the wives holding on by faith: Is anything too hard for the Lord? (Genesis 18:14)

Fern Chandler if the wife of 13 years to Darin Chandler. They are proud parents of two beautiful daughters; Jasmine and Faith. Originally from Philadelphia, Fern has now resided in Wilmington, Delaware for 15 years. She along with her husband are members and leaders of the Resurrection Center formally known as the Eighth Street Baptist Church. She was ordained to the office of Deacon in 2004 where she serves under the leadership of Bishop S. Todd Townsend and Pastor Cleo V. Townsend.

Fern has spoken passionately about the grace, mercy, and forgiveness of God toward women that have been through miscarriage as well as abortion. Even though parenthood is her biggest accomplishment to date, she is ready and willing to allow the Lord to lead and direct her into her destiny.

My Husband Is My High School Sweetheart
Missy Ross

My husband is my high school sweetheart. I first met him in 10th grade at a basketball game. I was a cheerleader and he was a basketball player from the opposing school. We officially started dating in our senior year. We dated through our first year of college but the long distance (him in New Jersey and me in New York) began to take its toll on the relationship. We reconnected in 2002 resumed our relationship and married 3 months later. I finally had my dreamboat back, grown up, matured, and satisfied. Mark and I always talked in depth about our values in life, desires, and dreams. So it was extremely hard for me to understand how and why he would marry me, knowing all the things I'd discussed with him about the damage alcoholism caused in my family and now he had the same problem.

I started noticing money missing out of the bank and finding bottles in my closet and in the garage. I even found a bottle under my car seat. Wait a minute, what is going on here? Mark is drinking? I confronted Mark with my findings and he stated, "I only drink socially after work with business associates." Signs of him using alcohol more frequently were becoming more apparent.

So here I am at the top of my game; spiritually, physically, mentally, personally, and professionally, in a marriage till death do us part and my God sent a spouse who was an alcoholic. NO WAY! This can't be!! See I was previously married twice. Although my first WASband fathered my two children and my second WASband introduced me to time sharing ownership, they were NOT WHO God had chosen as my Adam. Lord, I know I asked you if Mark was who you'd chosen for me. I prayed, we prayed together, and the answer was yes. How can You give me someone who has this problem? You know what I went through all my life. You know how many relatives and friends of mine had and still have this issue. The heartache that it causes, the nightmares that I still experience from past situations dealing with it, are you kidding me? Our blended family was in harmony from the very beginning of our marriage. Am I going to lose my new children? Is this going to set us all back?

A = agitated, aggravated; **L** = lost, lonely, **C** = callous, catastrophe, **O** = obligated, obvious, **H** = hurtful, hollow, **O** = overlook, outcast, outrage, **L** = lose life, loveless

This is how I was feeling all wrapped up inside of me every time I found out he was drinking.

Now he wasn't a sloppy alcoholic, you couldn't even tell when he was intoxicated. I knew because his actions weren't normal. My fear was that we were going to lose everything that we worked so hard for. Mark didn't work close to home and had to travel quite a distance to get to work. Was he going to drink and drive, ending up hurting himself or someone else? Denial set in. Mark didn't own up to him having an issue with alcohol because he still kept perfect attendance at work, he still received stellar evaluations and no one except for me would address the alcohol abuse. As he continued more, his health began to become affected. He had a couple of scares with his stomach and then one big scare with his heart. Now the medical staff on 2 different occasions had incidences on file for him with alcohol being a factor of the illness. I went into spiritual warfare, calling on my sistas to agree with me in prayer as we fought against the spiritual wickedness in the heavenly realm. I know what God said about my husband. He was my king, my protector, and we

162

were going to serve the Lord together in bringing people to him. After praying, I started doing research on alcoholism. I was surprised at some of the results that I found. The main one that stuck in my spirit was depression. Drinking alcohol can dull the mind to prevent a person from feeling. Was my spouse holding onto something that was causing him intense pain and to relieve it, he drank? What could be so devastating or traumatic that happened to him to cause him to run to the bottle when he thought about it?

It was time to address it head on. So I set up a date for us and was determined to listen and encourage him to go deep to find the root of this problem. My husband never dealt with the loss of his father who was his hero! He was strong for everyone else but never talked to anyone about how he felt about losing his dad; How it feels when Father's Day comes around, how he never grieved for him like he felt but always held back to be there for the rest of his family. Now the healing can begin. I wasn't going to judge him nor promote the alcohol use, but together, with the Lord, we were going to come out of this victorious!!! A few days later, he had a long discussion with this brother and another healing took place. He was able to grieve and his brother understood because it was his dad as well.

Now what do we do since the body is craving the alcohol? A couple of days after speaking with his brother, Mark's total healing and deliverance took place. While I was upstairs saying my prayers, he was down stairs calling out to the Lord. In his prayer closet, on his face, asking God to remove the taste and the side effects from alcohol from his body and mind. God did just that!!! The doctor wanted to give him some medicine to help his body adjust and get back to normal. The doctor also suggested he attend AA meetings. Well the medicine lasted for about a week and Mark only attended one AA meeting. No more pills, no more meetings!! He said he is going to rely on God and his wife who loved him and was going to be by his side praying and encouraging him that he can make it.

While sometimes now he still gets a little sad on Father's Day because he still misses his dad very much, I am able to be his strength and not let it get him down.

Alcohol has a new meaning for me now and I no longer struggle within for my family members, friends and most of all, my husband.

A = appreciate, assured, **L** = love, loyal, labored, **C** – Christ, covenant, committed, caring, **O** = one and only, obtainable, **H** = honest, humble, happy, harmonious, **O** = overjoyed, observant, **L**= laugh, like-minded

Here we are today, praising God for what he has done in our lives and being living testimonies to how loving one another, through the good times and the bad times, does pays off.

My king, Mark Lorenzo Ross!

 Missy Ross is a down to earth, woman of God, who loves to help wives accomplish their roles in being that "help meet suitable for him" that God intended them to be. She is a devoted wife of her high school sweetheart, Mark, mother of 5 (including 3 step children) and grandmother of 2. She lives in New Castle, Delaware and attends The Resurrection Center church in Wilmington, Delaware.

Beyond The Struggle: Crisis to Victory
Teresa Beasley

Robert and I have been married fifteen years. We live in a cozy ranch style home that we built on a pond surrounded by pine trees and one willow tree. We have both experienced successful careers and are active in the community. Robert also enjoys officiating youth and high school sports and in the past, it was typical for me to accompany him to the high school games. On our journey home, we'd laugh and talk about the game and, more often than we should have, found humor in the antics of the parents.

My life has always been one that was filled with activity–working long hours on the job as the leader of organizations where I lead and developed as many as sixty to eighty employees; as a licensed and ordained minister, serving at a large church; as volunteer mentor through the juvenile courts, serving as Chair and President on the local YWCA board; as the founder and ministry leader of ARMS for CHRIST, leading workplace and community Bible studies, preaching at women's events, as well as, providing encouragement and support to ARMS for CHRIST social media followers. I had a busy life doing good; after all, "busy doing good" is what society, and often even the church, deems as being successful, right?

In the spring of 2011, our lives suddenly changed when I was diagnosed with CIDP, a rare neuromuscular disease. The disease quickly progressed, leaving me with severe nerve damage, muscle weakness and numbness in my feet, legs, arms, and hands, impaired balance, and fatigue. The progressive nature of CIDP required me to commence ongoing IV infusions of six hours per treatment.

Wow! In a matter of a few weeks I went from the busy life doing good, to being unable to stand without losing my balance; losing the ability to tie my shoes, button blouses, and pull up zippers. Any functionality requiring the use of my thumbs and index fingers became nearly impossible. Being told that my tests results showed that I should be wheelchair bound and that they were amazed that I was managing to get around with the use of only a cane was staggering. Along with losing the physical ability, gone were our shared activities of going to the games together and date night.

It's not unusual to think of grief and loss as something experienced when a loved one dies; however, grief is experienced in life as a result of the loss of anything or anyone that leaves a devastating and unusually unexpected void. Though I have ministered to others experiencing grief, I didn't recognize until later, that as a result of this crisis, my husband and I were both experiencing grief and loss. Each of us was dealing with it in our own way, and, unfortunately, we dealt with it separate from one another.

For my husband, it was a loss of the wife he had been known to proudly describe as a strong black woman. To some extent, I believe it was the shock of seeing the level of vulnerability he was witnessing and neither one of us were in control of what was happening. For me, I had assumed the position that was the most comforting to me; that if I surrender all to the Lord I know I am in a win-win situation. "Lord, I know you are with me whether this side or on Heaven's-side. Jesus is my final answer."

On our way home after my first infusion I could sense how he felt. The disease was more severe than he had originally thought and he didn't see it coming. Over time, I'm sure there was the numbness of not knowing what to feel or what to do. I remember him asking me, "Why does he (the doctor) keep giving you the infusions if it's not making you better?" This question helped me to understand his unintentional denial that this condition was chronic—the ongoing infusions and that things might not return to "normal."

My focus shifted to those things that I was able to do and the environments or places that best enabled me to do them. The leadership at my place of employment, by the grace of God, gave me special privileges that allowed me to work flexible hours, as well as, from home when needed. I stepped away from the church where I served as an associate minister, resigned from board chair and president of the YWCA, and changed my volunteer status to inactive with the juvenile courts. I continued to minister, through ARMS for CHRIST, conducting weekly community and workplace Bible studies, encouraging followers through social media posts and responding to private mail, along with occasional preaching engagements. I did these things while I also continued infusion treatments and attended balance and physiotherapy.

Though I was not able to do all that I was once able to do, I still found myself busy doing good. That was until I noticed my husband was always angry, about anything, everything, or nothing. I noticed emotional outbursts that were directed at me, usually in response to attempts on my part to have a conversation because we had become so distant. He was in shut down mode and I was in doing good mode and all the while we drifted apart. Drifting only happens when you're not paying attention. It's like you're floating in the ocean and you're not paying attention to the shore line, drifting with the waves, and suddenly you look up and wonder how you ended up so far away from where you started. In our case, we weren't really paying attention to each other before the crisis, so when our participation in common activities stopped, we started to drift.

You might have picked up on this a little earlier in the story. When it comes to fight or flight behavior, my first instinct is flight. I would rather get very involved with "things" than to confront the situation at hand. So it stands to reason that my frustration level reached the point that I considered moving away. I wanted to go somewhere that would bring the same serenity that I had in my sunroom. It overlooks the pond and sits logistically under the willow tree, the place I love to sit and experience the manifested presence of God. Well, as God would have it, as I sat in that very room reading the Bible I came to a verse I had read and recited many times before, "God has not given us the spirit of fear, but the spirit of power, love, and a sound mind." That day it spoke clearly and personally to me! Thank God, He had given a name to the spirit so that we can more easily identify it. Relating this word to the commonly used acronym, F.E.A.R., False Evidence Appearing Real! The enemy was negatively impacting our marriage relationship through deception, using a skewed perception that was based on False Evidence Appearing Real (F.E.A.R., the spirit of deception.) I had to be reminded that the same spirit that raised Jesus from the dead lives in me. The spirit of power, love, and a sound mind, not the spirit of fear!

I had to step back from the F.E.A.R. to get a perspective that was different from my up close and personnel view. I needed a fifty-foot view. NO! I needed a God view! Up until the diagnosis of CIDP, I was busy being a human, doing. My workplace was pleased, my church was pleased, and the places I volunteered were pleased. I received certificates and plaques expressing their appreciation. Don't get me wrong, I know for a fact a positive impact was made through the word of God and through the ways in which God used me. It is awesome and sheer joy to see the move of God in our assignments. So much so, that we tend to want to cling to the places, persons, or things from our assignments even when God is ready to move us, expand us, and evolve us. God was moving me to shift my focus from merely a human doing to the human being He purposed me to be. Just as in Judges 4:4, "Deborah, a woman who was a prophetess and the wife of Lappidoth.." whom God used as a mouthpiece to speak to the people, yet did not take away from her position as the wife of Lappidoth. Teresa, a woman who is an ambassador for Christ and the wife of Robert, whom God has called to continue to proclaim His word, yet not take away from the position as the wife of Robert.

I have since, transitioned the workplace Bible study to a young lady I had been grooming;

I retired from my job, and now schedule ministry activities so that they don't interfere with family time.

As far as our progression through the stages of grief; we have come a long way, we are not where we used to be, and our hope is in knowing the best is yet to come! We've discovered new strengths in God, ourselves, and in each other. We've adapted to new patterns; we look to God for affirmation and not that of people regardless of their positions or titles, and we still enjoy helping others. The difference is now we live our life together and schedule other activities; whereas before we lived our activities and scheduled our life together.

It's important for you to understand that the facts of our crisis are still affecting us today. My mobility, hands, and balance are still impaired; I still deal with fatigue, and I still receive infusion treatments. The difference is our perspective, we see through a new lens. We no longer allow ourselves or each other to drift. What started as a crisis, now looks, feels, and lives like victory.

I am sharing my story with you in the hopes that the experience I gained through my crisis struggle, and eventual victory, can act as a launching pad that will propel you beyond the struggle of crisis and expedite your victory. Always remember, the manifestation of God's plan for our lives looks different than what we could ever imagine.

Forsaking
All Others and
Holding On to
One Another
Forevermore

A Word From
Gail Crowder

At a time when marriage is being redefined, considered "old-fashioned" and even worse, we all need a book like "Wives on Fire". As a marriage expert, I have partnered with Deidra Clark-Roussaw and TrulyWed Wives to promote wives projects and the responses from women have been unmatched anywhere else. Wives, especially Christian wives, are living in shame, judgment, and criticism, so they are suffering in silence. The "Wives on Fire" book is letting wives know that they are not alone and gives them the hope that they can overcome infidelity, addictions, and other challenges in their marriages with God's help. This book also prepares new wives who may face challenges and teaches them how to navigate life as being a wife. Deidra, and the other wives who are featured in this book, really makes it clear that wives appear to be more concerned about the wedding details than they are about the health and strength of the marriage for the long haul. Women reading "Wives on Fire" will be encouraged and inspired to be the kind of wife that God would have us to be so that we can have marriages that are pleasing to God. No matter the condition of your marriage, you will find what you need in "Wives on Fire" to keep your marriage healthy and strong.

Deidra Clark-Roussaw and TrulyWed Wives, thanks so much for such a transparent, thought provoking book. I know it will bless women and marriages for years to come.

Gail Crowder- The One Sexy Wife, Relationship/Lifestyle Expert, www.bsbconference.com, www.gailcrowderinc.com

A Word From
Martina Lambert

God designed marriage on purpose and his purposes are always good. God is the creator of marriage and the author of love. My prayer is that the women we will meet through their trials and triumphs will help impact our lives in such a way that we will understand God's Truth about the Covenant of Marriage. *Wives on Fire* will focus on the twists, turns, testimonies and miracles of our sisters' lives as a vehicle to help reshape our attitudes and actions in our marriages.

We embrace the emotions of our sisters who express their hurts, hopes, and expectations for a Godly marriage. May this book focus on the one and only true source the Lord Jesus Christ, who meets the needs of our hearts.

In a time when the Holy Spirit is grieved over the state of many marriages, I commend and support my daughter in the faith, sister, and friend, Deidra Roussaw, for providing a resource for women that will advocate reconciliation, restoration and romance in their marriages. Marriage is truly a mystery, so except the Lord builds a house we labor in vain.

From Barren to Bountiful
Asia Corbin

2 Corinthians 2:14 (KJV)

"Now thanks *be* unto God, which always causes us to triumph in Christ."

Praise be to God for He has made me glad. Through much hurt, pain, and confusion, I am standing victoriously in Christ. If I had to pick a woman in the Bible who personifies my testimony the most, I believe it would have to be Hannah. Hannah means 'God has favored me' (with a child). Hannah was a persistent woman.

My story begins with meeting my husband, who had custody of his sons from a previous marriage. Prior to meeting him, I secretly really did not want to visit or be around family or friends who had children or who were married.

Something inside of me felt inadequate. Let's face the truth, I was jealous, angry, and wanted children of my own. To make matters worse, I was a victim of my own selfish choices—I had two previous abortions. Subsequently, when I wanted children after I was married, I was told that I would not be able to have children due to a diagnosis of PCOS (Polycystic Ovary Syndrome). I have often felt that God was punishing me for what I had done. Every time I saw mothers with their children, a painful feeling of guilt and grief would overcome me. It had been four years since I was married, and still no child.

When I married my husband, I felt as though I walked straight into a fraternity, because it was all men, my husband and

3 boys who were way past puberty. Even the cat we had was a male. I thought, "What have I gotten myself into?" The toilet seat stayed up, causing me to fall in, not once but twice as I staggered to the toilet in the middle of the night. It was all PlayStation and X-Box games, and sports, as the boys played football and baseball. Just to make things even more manly, my husband was a dedicated football coach. I knew that I would never be able to tear him away from that. I felt all alone, in a world of testosterone and bravado.

I was harboring other feelings, that I was not a part of my husband unless I had a child by him. I was jealous of his children's mother. It was the blood factor. They all shared the same blood, but I did not. I felt so alone and left out. I would sit and watch how my husband interacted with his children. I would be angry with him because he was so devoted to them, yet at the same time, that was one of the qualities I absolutely adored about him.

As time went by, I began to feel more isolated. We were in our first year of marriage and I had not yet given my heart to the Lord. I was raised in an Islamic family and house. My father was an Imam (by definition, an Imam is an Islamic leadership position. It is most commonly in the context of a worship leader of a mosque and Muslim community by Sunni Muslims.)By the time I met Troy, I was not practicing Islam at all. In fact, I had rebelled against that religion and way of life totally. My husband was faithful to Christianity and attended church regularly without wavering. My feelings of anxiety and jealousy grew. I felt trapped.

My husband and I began to clash and the tension mounted. Of course, I called as many irate women as I could find to be on my side. Before long I left the house and moved into an apartment in Delaware. Troy did not ask me to leave, but he did not stop me either. I struggled to make sense of my life. In reality I was actually still confused and disoriented. I thought I would start all over, but it was easier said than done. My husband would call me periodically to talk.

I was still alone, thinking that it was ok because I was "independent". I had my own place, my own car, and a good job with the government. I thought that I had everything that I needed. It was almost true. I really couldn't go to my family because I married a Christian man. I was taught that if I left Islam I would die. All of my siblings and other family members were married and seemed to be happy. The truth was, I was barren. I had an empty home, an empty womb, and an empty heart.

Then it happened. One day my husband called and reminded me that I was a married woman. He asked me if I was finished playing around with our lives. I don't really know what happened but I told him that I would be right there, and I drove back to our house.

At first things didn't go very well. After a while, the truth finally sunk into my head and my heart that we were married, and we were one. I remember yelling at the top of my lungs as we were coming from dinner, "I am your wife!!! We are married."

I didn't realize it at the time, but God was drawing me to Himself. I began to go to church with my husband. It was all very strange to me because I had never had that experience before. Troy would explain certain things to me as he was now a Minister and had been saved for several years. He never pressured me to come to church or to convert. I believe this was because he too was a Muslim for many years. He just kept going and I began to follow him.

179

As I kept going and as Troy kept explaining things to me, I wanted to change, but I was afraid. Then one morning I was watching Creflo Dollar on TV. My husband had worked the overnight shift, and when he came home I told him that I wanted to come to Christ. He happily led me to Christ right there in the kitchen. Even though he had many Bibles, and a whole library of Christian literature, He hurried and bought me my first Bible. I was a women's Bible that he had inscribed for me and I still have it today.

I would be less than honest if I said that everything was perfect. I was still in competition for my husband's attention and affection. I was especially competing with Troy's youngest son, who still lived with us. He was a challenging child and by now he was 15 years old. He disrespected his father and me, and I wondered why Troy would not "lay hands on him and make him lie down in green pastures." I had had enough!

Troy and I finally sought counseling for us all. In the process, we went to a session at our church and I learned that our Lord Jesus Christ came from a blended family. Joseph was not His biological father, and He also had other half- brothers and sisters. I felt like Jesus knew my pain. I also learned several points about blended families. I learned that I should not call the children "Troy's sons" but instead call them our sons. As I took ownership of the boys, things began to change dramatically. There was still one problem. I desperately wanted a child from my husband and I was still barren. One Sunday I was so distraught about not having a child and I was scheduled to minister in dance. I prayed to God and I dedicated the dance to God. I poured my soul out to God and I ministered like never before.

The next week I went to work on a cold, snowy, and icy morning. As I tried to enter the building, I slipped on the ice. I was taken into the hospital for treatment and X-rays. As usual, before any x-rays are taken, women are asked if they are pregnant. I told the technician that I could not get pregnant, so there was no way that I could be. She took my urine and came back to the waiting room with the strangest look on her face. She told me I was pregnant according to the urine test. I respectfully told her that she didn't know what she was doing or what she was talking about. I called my husband who worked across the street from me and asked him to take me to a more reputable hospital. He picked me up and transported me to a well-known hospital, and helped me into the Emergency Department. As we went to the x-ray department, the same scenario played out. The tech took my urine and she too came back and said I was pregnant.

I didn't know whether to laugh or cry. I ended up doing both. It was in our 4th year of marriage that I conceived. I praised God like crazy. God heard me! He blessed me. Like Hannah, I dedicated my child to God. When we knew that it was a son, we named him Tobias (pleasing to God) Leron (My song, my joy).

Now as we are entering into our tenth year of marriage, many blessings have come our way. We had a beautiful daughter a year ago who we named Trinity, and we are now in ministry together. God is expanding our borders as we continue to seek His face and dwell in His presence.

My husband and I have moved to a place where we trust each other. I have also received the breakthrough that I so desperately needed, from family members who still tried to influence me with their spirit of Islam. I am free and have overcome many obstacles the enemy tried to place in front of me.

Like Hannah, I had my share of Penin'nahs in my life. Penin'nah means 'a precious stone', something like coral or pearl

181

- in other words, beautiful but hard and cold. I also have my Elkanah. Elkanah means 'bought/owned by God'. My husband is definitely owned by God and serves Him faithfully. And I also have my Samuel. Samuel means "God heard". My Tobias and Trinity are living proof that God hears when we pray. Today I am proud to know that all of my children, even though we are a blended family, share the same blood- The Blood of Christ.

I encourage you to keep seeking God's face and never give up hope. God is listening. Remember that there is purpose in everything God does, even if we don't see what it is. You are a gift to the world, and I pray that you come into the full maturation and manifestation of Jesus Christ.

Mrs. Asia Corbin, the revered wife and helpmate of Pastor Troy L Corbin Sr., is a native of Philadelphia, PA. Asia is a very down to earth woman of God, and is a true servant of God in many ways. She has been a member of Fresh Anointing Christian Center International since 2006, where she has served in the Medical Emergency Response ministry and also ministered in Mime Dance. After converting from Islam to Christianity, she has learned that her first ministry is unto the Lord. With the leading of the Holy Spirit, she then ministers to her husband Troy and their children, Tobias and Trinity. Asia faithfully serves by her husbands' side as First Lady in the newly founded, Fresh Glory of God Ministries in Wenonah, New Jersey.

Their goal is to advance the agenda of the Kingdom of God on the earth, while connecting, and reconnecting people to their Divine Identity, Purpose, and Power. Out of her passion and desire to help women and young ladies, "As I Am" Women's Discipleship Alliance was birthed in 2014. Many women of all ages and backgrounds come to her because of her transparency and willingness to nurture, and her warm Christian spirit. The scriptural basis of the ministry is the book of Ruth. Its concept is based on a two-fold paradigm. First, God will meet you just as you are. It doesn't matter what state you may be in, your past failures or victories. God is waiting with His arms open to embrace you, comfort you, strengthen you, encourage you and love you, right now in this very moment.

Secondly, as we learn to yield our hearts, thoughts, and lives over to God, we will blossom and become like God, and we will be "As I Am", which is one of the first ways God chose to reveal Himself to the Israelites. Asia believes that "As women we need to see ourselves as the Great I Am sees us". "We must mature and seek and stay in the presence of God in order to be transformed that we might be meet for the Kingdom of God and allow God to be glorified in us and through us".

In addition to her ministerial interests, First Lady Asia is very active in her son's School PTA and has worked as a Surgical Technician in several institutions across the nation.

My Blended Family
Diana Hill

According to the Merriam dictionary, a blended family consists of children who were born from a previous marriage or relationship. There were blended families during Biblical times. In Genesis 21 it shows how Abraham made a child with his wife, Sarah's, mistress, Hagar. The child's name was Ishmael. In Genesis 23, years later, it shows how Abraham and his wife made a child together. The child's name was Isaac. Eventually Hagar and Ishmeal had to leave Abraham's house. Another example is in Genesis 29 where Jacob had children by two different wives. Their names were Leah and Rachel. He also had children with his mistresses Bilah and Zelph. In the blended family struggle love and faith will surely conquer all.

My name is Diana Hill and I have been with my husband for 17 years and married for 9 ½ years. My husband has six children and 18 Grandchildren. I don't have any children of my own. His children's ages are from 20-32; five girls and one boy. I love all of my stepchildren. It wasn't hard to love my husband's children. I came from two blended families. I have a stepmother and a stepfather; both showed me love and compassion. They both gave me understanding even when my biological parents didn't understand. My stepparents were my example of how to love even through challenges and struggles. Being a stepparent can be just as challenging and rewarding as being a wife.

The foundation of my blended family stems from my solid marriage. My marriage is built on Godly principles, love for one another, understanding, forgiveness, commitment, selflessness, and open communication. We show that we are a unit of one. When difficulties appear between the children and me, the spirit of God and the love we have for one another outweighs all of it.

The dynamic of me being a stepmother had its challenges. I had to learn how to navigate through six different personalities as they come from a different upbringing. Some of my stepchildren are affectionate while others aren't. Respect, trust, and communication had to be built. I had to learn how to understand instead of being understood. At times it can be difficult. Dealing with children that were raised differently than me requires patience. There have been situations where I have been told by all of them that "I am not their mother and I cannot tell them what to do or, this is my dad's house!" During these times a rift had begun between my husband and me. I had to lean on God for strength. God always gave resolve even when I didn't think the outcome was fair. I also learned that respect for and towards them was far more important that me trying to be their friend. This also taught me that this is the same way that a natural mother feels about her children.

I made some mistakes, had to lower some standards, and had to admit that I had some insecurities that stemmed from not having children of my own. I was overbearing. One of my biggest mistakes was thinking we would all be one happy family right away. I had to realize that that would not happen overnight. There were times when I cried because I couldn't believe that I was able to love children that weren't my own. The grace of God gave me strength to love my husband's children as my own. I had to gain knowledge and wisdom that some of our conflict came from my husband not being with their mom. Some of the power struggle was within them and they had things they needed to come to grips with.

All of my stepchildren have lived with us in different stages of their lives. The joy of being a stepmother is rewarding and it comes in different forms. I was able to see all of the children evolve from child hood to young adult hood and to adults. I was beside their parents at births, graduations, and proms. I even celebrate with them when some got their new homes. I love giving of myself, my time, and my joy. I love spending time with my grandchildren. I have a garden in my back yard and I love every year when some of my grandchildren help with the weeds and help me plant. I love when we cook together or when I show them a new recipe and we all prepare it together for the first time. I am blessed to know all of my grandchildren from birth.

The Holy Spirit showed me how to have selflessness. One example occurred in 2006 when one of my stepdaughters had to deliver a still born child on the eve of my mother's funeral. I was at the hospital with her until 3:30 in the Morning. My soul was hurt and I was weak, but God gave me strength to be there for her until the ordeal was over. Hours later my husband and I buried my mother.

Another happened in 2013 when one of my stepdaughters and I had a big fallout. She lived with us and the outcome of the situation caused her to leave the house. The very next Sunday I obeyed the Holy Spirit. God put it in my heart to tell her to come back home and that I didn't need to have an apology. This is the kind of love a mother has for her children. The Holy Spirit also told me not to bring the situation up ever again. I had a discussion with my husband and she came back home. That act was the beginning of the turning point of our relationship. The respect she has for me today is much better.

I am blessed to be able to have a cordial relationship with my stepchildren's mothers. Today our lines of communication are open. This developed over time. In the beginning of my relationship with my husband, before marriage, I was not met with open arms. I understand today that my stepchildren's mothers were being protective over their children and protective over the relationship they had with my husband. As my relationship with my husband progressed the relationship with their mothers grew better. This was a long and hard process due to the feelings that they still had for my husband. My husband showed his children's mothers that he was in love with me and that he intended on being with me for the rest of his life. The biggest declaration took place after we got married. My husband publically acknowledged that I was his children's stepmother. I officially became a part of their lives. I can honestly say that my children's mothers and I have the utmost respect for each other. If I am going through with something, none of them get in the middle or choose sides.

I have the heart to love children who are not my own. The years of being a stepmother have given laughter, joy, tears, and pain. God has shown me how to humble myself when dealing with my stepchildren. I have learned how to deal with the rudeness and occasional dislikes from them. I have learned how to find solutions during power struggles. There are times when they hurt I hurt with them. I have and still will cry with them. I try to give the best advice that I can. I also try my best to up lift the Lord to them. God has given me grace to be able to stand on the back burner if need be for them and He has given me strength even when I want my flesh to intervene. My flesh does at times but I have learned to put my flesh under subjection. My home is a stable environment because of the love I have. I may argue and fuss with my stepchildren but I love them all. Most of all, the love that my husband and I show each other makes it much easier to deal with every day challenges that come with being a stepmother. I, Diana Hill, am the glue to my family. At the end of the day, I know my stepchildren love me as well.

1 Samuel 1:19 talks about how Hannah, who was Samuel's mother, was barren in her womb. She prayed to God daily. 1 Samuel tells us that Hannah did conceive a child, who was the Prophet Samuel, and she dedicated his life to the Lord.

In the beginning of my marriage I can say I was like Hannah. My marriage was troubled. I gave myself to the Lord. I started serving in God's house and I changed my whole life around. Within a year God answered my prayers. My marriage was restored, shaped, and molded to God's will for a healthy marriage. I thank God for being like Hannah.

In the book of Acts, it talks about Priscilla, who was the wife of Aquila. They were followers of Paul with the first churches. Priscilla and her husband were both evangelists. It is also known that she is one if the authors in the book of Hebrews. So in 2015 I can compare myself to her because I am a follower of Jesus, my husband is a deacon in church, and an armor bearer to our Bishop. I am a teacher of new member's class in my church, I serve in evangelism, and I also serve as an Usher. Today, like Pricilla, I am a co-author of this amazing book where my testimony will help other wives in their marriage who deal with the same situation.

Diana Hill was born and raised in Philadelphia Pa. Diana is a student at Temple University. She has been married to Tyrone Hill for 9

1/2 years. Diana has six stepchildren and 18 grandchildren. Currently she is an Independent business operator for Total Life Changes. Diana attends Abundant Life Healing Fellowship Church in Philadelphia, Pa. She serves on different ministries including a co department head for Sure Foundation. She serves as an Usher and is also a servant on evangelism. Diana's passion in life is to serve God and to serve people. Her mission is to uplift the marriage between husband and wife. Currently Diana serves as one of the Administrators for Wives with Lives, a Facebook group.

My Boaz
Gwendolyn Drummond

It was February 15, 2006...one of the darkest days in my life: The death of my father and my marriage. As I walked down the long corridor of the hospital after watching my father take his last breath, I was numb from grief. I could hear voices around me, but they seemed so far away. I walked to the garage, got into my car, and turned on the radio, playing was Luther Vandross' "Dance with My Father." I was so overwhelmed, and I began to cry to the point that I was hyperventilating. I pulled out my asthma inhaler and took a few puffs and just sat there until I could muster up the energy to drive home and tell my children that their grandfather, who they loved and adored, was gone.

I started thinking about how my life would be forever changed. How would I function? How would I overcome the grief and loneliness that I would experience? Who would be there to comfort me?

I arrived to my home and put the key in the door. My hands were shaking so much that I could barely unlock the door. My legs began to wobble, and all I could think was, "Lord, please let me get in this house. I know my husband will be waiting for me at the door and catch me when I fall."

I opened the door to a dark living room and no one there waiting for me. I climbed the stairs to find my husband lying in the bed, watching television. I fell on the bed. I couldn't wait until he wrapped his arms around me to tell me everything was going to be all right, but he never touched me or said anything to me.

My son could hear me sobbing, so he came into the room and hugged and rocked me. My husband got out of the bed, got dressed, and left the house. He came back twenty minutes later with my mother. He looked at me and said, " I didn't know what to do". At that moment, I realized that if he couldn't be there for me at one of the most devastating and difficult times in my life that he wasn't the man that God intended for me to have.

I remembered watching T.D. Jakes one morning as he preached about marriage and relationships. He stated that "you would know if that person was meant for you if you could imagine him or her standing by your side when they lowered your mother in the grave." Six months later, after fourteen years of marriage, we were divorced. During those fourteen years, we had our share of ups and downs. We had two children each from previous relationships. There was not a significant gap in age difference and the children seemed to get along well. His parents had been married since they were eighteen years old. They were always having family gatherings. This was what I wanted for my family.

When we first started dating, everything was going great. We were so in love. We spent every waking moment we could together. Then I noticed some things that didn't sit well with me, like he loved hanging out and drinking with his friends. He lived with his parents and only paid them fifty dollars every two weeks. When I asked him what he wanted to do with his life, he said, "I'm not sure yet."

At thirty years old, you're not sure yet? Red flags were flying all over the place. I overlooked a lot of things because I was "in love." The red flags didn't matter to me. I kept saying to myself that things would get better…after all, if he loves me enough, he will change. Four years into the relationship, we decided to get married. I had just purchased a home and now I was going to have a "real" family and someone to spend the rest of my life with. Things could only get better, I thought. I was always a church-going, bible-believing person, but was in a backslidden state. I never talked with the Lord about what I should be looking for in a husband. I never even talked with Him about my readiness to be a wife. After all, how hard could marriage be? His parents and my parents made it look easy.

We were so excited, preparing for the big day. The morning of the wedding, everything that could go wrong seemingly went wrong. I experienced a bad bout of stomach cramps and diarrhea and could hardly stand up. The limousine driver was late picking me up, and then I couldn't find the keys to lock up the house. This was not how I wanted to start my new beginning. Well, that's exactly how it started and ultimately ended. The love, trust, respect, loyalty, and concern diminished year after year.

I was not blameless in the situation. I didn't fully understand my role as a wife and helpmeet. I was not living for the Lord, so I became frustrated trying to "fix" the situation apart from God. "Cast your cares on the Lord and he will sustain you; he will never let the righteous be shaken." Psalm 55:22 (NIV).

I couldn't pray for my husband or marriage because I was too angry and hurt. I felt that I wasted so many years to end up in this place in my life. My heart became hardened and I was miserable. I reasoned with myself that it was probably meant for me to be alone or that I was too independent to come under subjection to a man. After all, I was the "breadwinner."

After the divorce, I vowed never to get married again. I became involved in a few relationships afterwards, but they were wrong on so many levels. My prayer to the Lord was to help me find a good man. I was a good "catch" and I "deserved" a good man. I didn't want to live my life alone, but I was looking for happiness in all the wrong places. I was so empty inside.

I began to question God: "Why can't I find a 'good' man that will love me unconditionally and accept me for me? Lord, where is my Boaz?' I could clearly hear the Lord's voice, "Because you asked Me to help you, but you keep getting in the way."

"For I know the plans I have for you, declares the Lord, plans to prosper you and not to harm you, plans to give you hope and a future" Jeremiah 29:11 (NIV).

In January 2009, after being divorced for three years and having no future husband in sight, I made the decision to rededicate my life to the Lord and live for Him. I knew that true happiness and peace can only be found in Him. I joined a church, swore off men, stopped drinking socially and hanging out, paid my tithes faithfully...and then all hell seemed to break loose. The devil was busy at work, attacking my children, family, finances, and stability. But what he really wanted, he seemed to be getting, for my faith to waver.

I couldn't understand why this was happening to me. The Lord says, "I am come that they might have life, and that they might have it more abundantly," John 10:10 (KJV). I decreed and declared that devil was a liar and he would not have me, my family, finances, or most importantly, my faith. I began to get more into the Bible and my prayer life increased. Although I had the faith of a mustard seed, I still had it and I could feel that soon, I would be seeing the manifestation of His promises, but in His time.

Nevertheless, trial after trial after trial came. I could see no end in sight. I was beginning to lose my focus at work. I was more preoccupied with the problems I was having than giving it to God. Nothing is impossible with Him, but I was having a really hard time believing it. My faith was being tested and I knew it. If I could just hold steady and fast to His Word, I knew

194

my stormy season would pass. Every day, all day, I would just keep saying, "Help me, Lord".

It was a rainy evening on March 28, 2012, and I was on my way to meet my date. He was a pretty nice guy that I had known for some years. It was his birthday and we were going out to dinner. I was running late, as usual, and I had less than a quarter tank of gas. Any other time, I would be driving on fumes, but something said, "You'd better stop for gas."

I pulled into the Hess gas station and ran inside to pay for my gas. When I came out, there was a big red truck blocking me in. I was thinking to myself, "Not today...I'm so not in the mood for this." I saw this guy standing there with his hands in his pockets, staring at me. He was fine, but looked a little young. He said, "Hey, do you need somebody to pump that gas for you?" I said, "No, I need somebody to pay for it". He said, "I can do that, too". And from that day forward, he has never left my side.

I finally felt like a "woman." He helped me through some trying times. He was someone who I trusted. I felt safe with him. He always kept his word and he took care of my heart like no other man ever has. He was so in tune with me that he knew when I needed to go to the bathroom. It sounds crazy, but it is so real.

We both had children and our families blended together so well. What I loved most about him was his love for the Lord. Finally, a man I could be equally "yoked" with. A year later, in April, he proposed, and the following year we were married. He gave me the wedding of my dreams. We had a beautiful beach wedding in Punta Cana, Dominican Republic, surrounded by family and friends. He was everything I've always wanted, "my Boaz," sent from heaven. The Lord finally answered my prayers. We were on an emotional high and we were never coming down...right? WRONG.

Struggles and problems that we never imagined could happen in the marriage began to happen. We both suffered from broken marriages and as much as we tried not to allow that to have an impact on our relationship, it did. We never fully released the hurts of our past and they were coming back to haunt us so much that we were using the "D" word divorce.

We are both very strong-willed, caring, and loving people who had been hurt. You know the old cliché "hurt people, hurt people?" That was becoming a reality in our marriage. We argued so much and with so much rage that we started looking different to one another. Neither one of us wanted to give in. We built a wall of anger, bitterness, unforgiveness, disrespect, and distrust that would probably have taken a lifetime to tear down. I had never cried so much in my life. I was totally depending on my husband for my happiness.

But we see every day in our lives that people will disappoint you all the time. The hurt and anger was so real that we couldn't even pray for one another. We seem to have forgotten how important we were to one another and were just focused on ourselves individually. Had the love and passion we had for one another fizzled out already? Did the Lord really send him to me? Lord, please, I can't have another failed marriage. We needed help in the worst way.

One day while on Facebook, I stumbled across an organization called TWOgether Marriages, founded by Dwight and Deidra Roussaw. I reached out to Deidra and our lives were forever changed. Their vision, passion, and commitment to marriage is unsurpassed. I was one (as was my husband) that didn't think we needed any counseling. After all, that's the profession I'm in. Surely I can do this on my own. But I couldn't.

They counseled my husband and I from a biblical perspective with love and objectivity. They never took sides or judged us. They helped us realize why we first fell in love and decided to get married. But most of all, they encouraged us to focus on God and His promises and the marriage wouldn't fail.

I realized also that I was not where I needed to be in Christ or my prayer life, and that's why I gave into my flesh when troubles arose between my husband and I. There are always going to be troubles because the enemy wants to destroy marriages. Marriages are ordained by God and that's why we need Him in every aspect of it.

I stopped asking God to change my husband. Instead, I asked Him to change me. When disagreements came about, I didn't argue. Instead, I got my Bible and started reading the Word and praying. Someone has to be mature in the relationship. I also continued to do my wifely duties, even in the midst of chaos, and I noticed that it softened his heart more.

We rededicated our lives and our marriage back to the Lord. My husband is my best friend, and I'm just as madly in love with him as I was in the beginning. We keep God in every aspect of our lives and go to Him with every decision we make regarding our lives. We realize that we can do nothing apart from God. We also make sure that we have daily devotions. My husband covers our family in prayer every morning before he leaves for work. We have special nights where we study from powerful books like Power of a Praying Husband and Power of a Praying Wife by Stormie Omartian and Spouse-ology by Juanita and Chris Gissentaner. These books provided helpful insights on having a lifelong, loving, and Christ-centered marriage.

We make sure that we take time out to go on a date every week. We travel and take long road trips together. Our road trips are the best because it's just us and we get to talk and learn more about one another. There's nothing more beautiful than driving down I-95, listening to jazz and talking to your best friend. We talk with one another throughout the day just to say, "I love you and I'm thinking about you".

We are learning to fight fair -- no name calling, shaming, or blaming. We worship together. We also involve ourselves with activities that promote Christian marriages. It's an awesome feeling to be around other couples who want to grow their marriage. If you don't feed your marriage, it will surely die.

Divorce is not an option for my husband and me. We will not allow the enemy to destroy it. We are committed to one another and our marriage. As long as he follows Christ, I will follow him. We will continue to seek the Lord's face in every trial and tribulation because they will come, but we will face them together.

Remember to keep God first in your marriage and it will last. My favorite verse for wives is Ecclesiastes 4:12: "Though one may be overpowered, two can defend themselves. A cord of three strands is not quickly broken."

The wife of the Bible that I feel that I am most like is "Ruth". Ruth was young Moabite widow (a foreigner who did not follow the Hebrew God) that was married to Naomi's son Mahlon for 10 years. After the death of Mahlon Naomi told Ruth to return to her mother. However Ruth who was devoted and loyal tells Naomi "Where you go I will go, and where you stay I will stay. Your people will be my people and your god my god. Where you die I will die, and there I will be buried. May the Lord deal with me, be it ever so severely, if even death separates you and me." Ruth was faithful. She exemplified dedication and love.

Ruth had no man to provide for her. When Naomi suggested to Ruth that she go to the threshing floor and call upon the nearest male relative to serve as her kinsman-redeemer who would buy back their dead husband's land and become Ruth's new husband, she went that evening and encountered Boaz. Boaz didn't have first rights to her but he gave the one who did an opportunity to buy the land and marry Ruth but he was only interested in the land so he opted out of both. Boaz then married Ruth.

Boaz was very protective of Ruth. He accepted all of the baggage that came with her. Boaz gave Ruth extraordinary treatment. He was respectful and had the character of God. Boaz was not merely interested in Ruth's physical beauty but her noble character. Through their union Ruth was able to find a newfound faith in God. Ruth was a witness of God's promise that he will never leave or forsake you.

Weight Management Coach

"What, do you know that your body is the Temple of the Holy Spirit which is in you, which you have of God and you are not your own? For you are brought with a price: therefore, Glorify God in your body, and in your spirit which are God's."

1 Corinthians 6:19-20

Gwendolyn Drummond married her best friend, Fred, on July 22, 2013. They reside in Philadelphia and are the proud parents of four adult children and two grandchildren. In her spare time she enjoys exercising, reading, and traveling with her husband. She holds a Master's of Social Work degree from

Widener University and a Bachelor's of Science in Health Policy and Administration from Penn State University. She is passionate about serving vulnerable families and children.

Gwendolyn possesses strong leadership skills as it relates to courage, self-awareness, and determination. Her work has allowed her to broaden and deepen her understanding as it relates to building effective relationships.

She accepted Christ at a young age while worshiping at Deliverance Evangelist Church and is currently a member of Redeemed Worship Center Church under the leadership of Dr. Rosa Drummond. She is active in their marriage fellowship.

Within the past year she has adopted a healthy lifestyle which has been a challenge for her in the past. In addition to clean eating, she attends boot camp 4 times a week under the leadership of David A. Miller for Good Bodies and Temple Building Fitness. She also takes a spin class weekly that she enjoys with her husband.

There are times of hardship and trials that can threaten a marriage. She understands the importance of setting aside time daily as couples to pray together and read God's word. Although two are stronger than one, a marriage joined together under God and built on His promises and Word is stronger.

Her favorite scripture is "Though one may be overpowered two can defend themselves. A cord of three strands is not quickly broken" (Ecclesiastes 4:12).

Blended Family
Laverne Cheeseboro

It was always in me to be a wife. By the time I was fourteen, I knew what kind of wedding I would have and who would be in it. I had my first experience of "write the vision; make it plain" and didn't even know it. Now I can say that due to life circumstances in my young life, my desire to become a mother came before marriage. I guess in my mind; it was easier to make the baby. While my grandma was stern about me not having any babies before I graduated high school and got married, I began to develop a mind of my own or maybe a mind of rebellion.

So by eighteen, God gave me my heart's desire, my first baby boy. He was no accident, but surely planned too soon. My relationship with his father was tough. My pregnancy was tough. My grandma insisted on not bringing a baby in the world unwed. I was sure at that moment that we needed to wait. All I knew was I wanted to be a mother, have my children by one man, and be married. Yep, in that order. Backwards, you say?

Now, after ups and downs, five years later, we did it again. This time, we tried for the girl; this time, planning the wedding. God gave me my baby boy. With more ups and downs, still no wedding. As a matter of fact, it was division at its best. He went to jail. Three years later, the most devastating thing happened. Three weeks after he came home, he was murdered, leaving me with an eight-year-old and a three-year-old to raise alone.

My desire to be married remained, even with a broken heart and clueless as to whom, when, and how I would be web. Learning from my grandma, Bible study, mentors, and reading books, I began to prepare to be a wife. My grandma didn't really support men around the boys and I wasn't comfortable with it either, especially if marriage wasn't possible. Men will show their true feelings from the tolerance levels they have with the kids. Do they really care and accept them? Are they safe with and around them?

Because of my own childhood, I was very careful... more like extremely overprotective. I began to be focused on being a whole woman for the whole man I would be married to, my Boaz. I don't think I ever really thought of having a father for my boys. I was not interested in replacing their father and not interested in possible adoption from another man, but I knew a husband was important. I wasn't even sure of whether I wanted to have more children because I didn't want different fathers for my children...even more with their father being gone.

As time went on, I met my now-husband. He professed his love for me, put so much desire and care in my children, and showed that he wanted to be a part of our lives. Not just mine...ours. I paid attention and prayed. My grandma was totally against anyone coming in and "acting like their father." He was a great man for us. He loved me; he loved the boys. He didn't have any children, so to me that was a plus. I felt that because he didn't have children and they didn't have their dad, they were a blessing for one another. All the while, seeds were being planted in my boys' heads that he was not their father. My boys were six and eleven.

We took the time out to get to know each other. I watched how he interacted with the boys. He was good with them, especially teaching them about life as a young boy and how to become a man. He even taught them manners and respect. There were things they just didn't learn being raised by women. While single, I lived with my grandma and aunt. When it came to holding them accountable, teaching them, and spending time with them, we did it together. I would always ask my boys whether they were okay with him, if they liked him, and how did they feel about him being around. They would tell me that he was cool. They liked him. They were okay with us getting married. I prayed, we went to premarital counseling and jumped the broom.

My baby boy was three when his father passed away so he started losing memory of him. My husband filled the void for him because memory-wise, he's the only man in his life. My oldest was eight. He never forgot his dad and in the back of his mind would never let anyone take his place. He kept it silently tucked away. His withdrawal and rebellion weighed on us heavily, but my husband was and is still in it to win.

I always took my son to therapy and encouraged him to journal to deal with his feelings, not to keep them bottled up. Even in that, he was very reserved. Eight years together and four years married, I took his electronic devices. At nineteen, my son finally wrote and expressed his true feelings for my husband, confessing he didn't like him and didn't appreciate him disciplining them, telling me they lied to me about wanting me to marry him. My heart shattered. I cried for days.

On one hand, I could've taken it to mean that he was angry so he said these things to hurt us, but on the other hand, I couldn't because he didn't know we would find and read what he wrote…or maybe he did. I was always hesitant to talk to them about their dad, so I waited until they asked. My oldest never asked, so it was time for us to talk and to help him understand blessings. He stated clearly, "That n***a will never be my father!" My husband was so hurt. I just knew this would tear our family apart.

My husband didn't know if he should stay or leave, if he should keep trying or back off. He was at a loss. All I knew is that I wasn't going to stand for division in my home. All I knew was to offer forgiveness and work on things. So I called a counselor at the church. I have always allowed my children to express their feelings. After all, they are human and feel just like adults do, so I listened to them. I didn't just excuse their behavior and words as invalid.

After all these years together, this is when I began to learn about the blended family. It can be perfect or it can be a hot mess. I remember someone telling me they waited until their child was grown to get married because they didn't like being a part of a blended family and it literally broke their mother and her husband up. My mother was married, so I knew what it was like to live in a blended family. My stepfather loved me and protected me like I was his own.

I never imagined my family being broken and torn. There was so much tension in our home. There was so much pain in our home. It didn't look like there was any healing in sight at all. In between my tears, all I could do was call on God, stepping in the middle of my husband and man-child exchanging unpleasant words I had never imagined. One thing in my mind, though, was that I would never take a man over my kids…not even my husband. I would never allow anyone to hurt them. Even though they may be wrong, they were children… my children.

In all of this, I learned so much, yet I still didn't know what I missed. I was so wrapped up in my son being rebellious because he never got over losing his father that I never once thought that his reasons included me being married or who my husband was. That question never came across my mind. I was so hurt as to why he lied to me. He said he wanted me to be happy. This was so hard. I wasn't about to let the devil have my family, period.

I learned that the seeds were planted from day one of my husband being over to meet the family. "He's not your father!" My son held on to that and never let it go. My husband made it clear he would never attempt to replace their father, but he embraced them, took on being in my life to raise them, and called them sons. While my husband was never a threat, I always saw him as one. I thought that when I got married I was whole, but marriage brings out things that were once way down at the bottom up to the surface. My overprotection for my boys stemmed from experiences way back in my childhood. I expected my boys to embrace someone who I didn't even fully trust and he wasn't even a threat.

So before I decided to even have children, the seed was planted, and before I got married, the seed was planted in my children. My fears were all over the atmosphere of our home and life. I always put an emphasis on "my kids"…we were married and they were "MY KIDS!" I learned in counseling that I remained a single mother in my marriage and my husband never felt he was truly a part of parenting them. While he called them sons, during disagreements, they became "your kids." I was comfortable stepping in and cutting him off in front of the boys. While I would never let my boys play us against each other, I would go against him in front of them.

Four things we experienced in our blended family were the seeds being planted, my fears and extreme overprotection filling in the atmosphere, our language confirming his position in their lives, and going against my husband in front of our kids. We definitely needed help. We had some responsibilities to accept. We needed some growth and maturity as a blended family, and we needed to begin the forgiveness and healing process in order to make it work.

There are things in our lives that we are in control of, but all we do is still according to God's will for us. This is where the blended family even started for me. I am the only child of my parents and I never saw them together. My husband is the only child of his parents. He saw his parents together, but not married. His mother and father had other children and were married to others; my parents had other children and were married to others. We didn't see the importance of having children after marriage and we both grew up in church. This was the first seed planted.

While my grandmother stressed over and over again not to have any babies before I graduated high school, not to have any children from guys in the neighborhood -- she even told me not to have children by a man who already had children -- not one time did she say that I should get married and have children with my husband, in that order. The funny thing is that while I may not have heard it from her, I watched her model it. My grandma was with one man all her life who gave her five children.

Now don't get me wrong... life was as it was for me. You may say, "Well, what if you did get married to your son's father and then he passed away? Life happens. Divorce happens. "Things happen that can and will very well open the door for blended families, and in some cases, this is truly a blessing.

I saw my husband as a blessing for sure. He didn't have any children and my children didn't have their father. He and I shared so much in common that I saw that God knows what He is doing! Even in all of that, the tests and challenges came along the way. Why? Because Satan has a goal and motive in mind...division of the family! The minute my husband professed his love for me and I became his wife and I felt it was time for him to meet my boys, Satan stepped in to stop it!

My family hated the thought of bringing a man into their lives and especially permanently, someone who "thought he was their father," based on their perception. My children heard people say, "You're not their father!" or "He ain't their daddy!" so many times that my oldest absorbed it like water flowing through his body.

As time went on, things happened that were an attempt to destroy what we were establishing, but we managed to stick it out. People will plant seeds in your children's life. The resentment grew in my oldest son. Being in a blended family became very challenging and sometimes painful for my husband.

Growing up, there was dysfunction and abuse in my life from verbal, emotional, physical, and poor parenting sources. I thought that by the time I was married, I was healed and whole for sure. I learned a lesson that day! Sometimes, we bury things and when we come to certain roads in our life's journey, those bones are dug up.

I remember saying how I would never let this and that happen to my children because I always felt I wasn't protected as a little girl, so I would set rules with my husband: Don't talk to them, don't punish them, and don't do anything unless I approve it. If he would ask them questions or talk to them, I would step right in. I would speak for them, defend them, and give my husband the business about "MY KIDS." It got to the point that my husband would say, "I'm done." He would say, "I can't win. You don't respect me in front of them, and you make me second to them." He had so many feelings, reacting to my behavior and attitude. So there you have it…another seed. He would say to me, "You deal with YOUR KIDS!" This is where my fear and overprotection kicked in and inspired the division in our home. This is also where our language spoke life over our blended family.

As time went on, the challenges became overwhelming. My son stood by his feelings of my husband never being his father.

He would barely talk to him. He didn't want to spend time with him. Division was in our home and affecting our marriage. One of the first good things about this all was that I began to grow closer to God. I needed Him like never before! We needed Him!

I asked God to give us what we needed to get through. God gave us the resources we needed to learn, grow, and heal from all the craziness. We learned how to pray together instead of fighting against one another. We were on the same team and we shared the same vision with the same goals in mind. We received counseling and learned how to communicate so that there was no more "my" and "your".

Let me tell you... my husband always called them "son," so he would still say to me "MY SON." Now, when we talk, we use "OUR." It takes time to develop this habit, but the more you say it and hear it, the better it feels, so you look forward to it. Even in our disagreements, we maintain that language. It reminds us we are one, even in the reality that they are not his biological children. The boys can't play us against one another. God began to give us married friends that were also in blended families. We were able to see the models of how the blended family could work and be a good thing. Having support and counseling is very helpful when having a blended family.

A lot of us have childhood memories and issues that may resurface in our lives. It is best to communicate those feelings to your spouse. Be comfortable telling your husband about your fears and worries and where and what they stem from. This allows for the real healing in your life. It also allows trust and good communication to be strengthened in your marriage. We learned how to submit to one another in areas that we were weak in when it came to the children. I did not know how to teach them to be a man, and my husband wasn't responsible for nurturing them the way I am. We learned how to balance one another out and hold each other up when things became stressful or overwhelming. We came together when important decisions need to be made. We encouraged each other when we felt like we are failing as parents. Having a college-aged young adult child and a teenager surely comes with challenges. Bringing someone in as head of household and "father" can be traumatic to some children. Adults may see the blessing in it, but children don't understand that yet.

I often wonder where the testimonies in my life are. I sometimes struggle to see them, but I am so grateful to call this a testimony. While Satan can attempt to kill, steal, and destroy, the one key thing "we grew up in church" remembering is to go to our main source. GOD allowed us to get through everything, so we give God the glory in the blended family.

Laverne Cheeseboro is a wife of five years, a mother of two boys, twenty and fifteen, and resides in Philadelphia, PA. After four years of dating, Laverne and her husband, Derrick, married in June, 2010. At a young age Laverne was caring for her siblings and by age 14 she was caring for her grandmother, helping her around the house, going with her to doctor appointments, and caring for her when she was sick. She always had a love for helping and caring for people.

Laverne was raised in church by her grandmother. She was baptized at age 12 and became a member of Cornerstone Baptist Church. Throughout her teen years she battled with her spiritual life and religion. In 2003, Laverne was invited to church with a co-worker and on Easter Sunday she accepted Christ as her personal savior on her own. Her faith was immediately tested when in July, 2003 the father of her children was murdered. This was when life began to change for her as she knew it. Finally Laverne decided to seek what God called her to be and do.

In High School, attending Bok Technical Vocational, her trade was Cosmetology, where she currently specializes in braiding hair. In 2005 she went to school to train to become a Nurse Assistant. In 2009, Laverne graduated from Kaplan University with her Associates degree in Medical Office Management with plans to attend nursing school. After getting married, Laverne's faith was once again tested. After receiving the devastating blow that she could no longer have children, instead of becoming angry with God, this time she began to seek him more to find what God wanted to get from this. Laverne is the now the Owner and Provider of Heavenly Made Creations Family Child Care and pursuing her bachelor's degree in Early Childhood Education.

Currently Laverne is a member and Vine leader of a Philadelphia Chapter of Whine & Cheese, an organization where women meet once a month to socialize, uplift, encourage, and support one another. Laverne is also a member of the Red Hat Society. She is a team leader of the TrulyWed Wives Ministry and lead administrator of a Facebook group, Wives with Lives. In 2012, Laverne was baptized and received the right hand of fellowship at Enon Tabernacle Baptist church. Laverne and her husband attend the Not Easily Broken Marriage ministry.

"It is my passion to help women. It is my passion to love and take care of children and seniors. Helping and taking care of people makes my heart happy. I will always go where the Holy Spirit leads me to do God's Will."

Keeping God in Your Marriage and Everyone Else Out...So You Say!
Nicole S. Green

Not until a couple years into our marriage did I find exactly the true meaning of keeping God in our marriage. My husband Keith and I were told about it during premarital counseling, speaking with other Christian couples and family members who expressed this important idea, but it did not stand out to us. It was not until my father's speech at our wedding reception that it became most valuable. I guess this was because I was a product of my parents' marriage and I witnessed what a marriage could look like firsthand by being in the same household. I often wondered how my parents still wanted to stay with each other after certain incidents within their marriage. There was my answer...keep God in your marriage!

In April of 2012, just months before some of the most important events in our life together, the unthinkable happened...my relationship with my mom and only sister came to a screeching halt. Unfortunately, I can honestly say I actually do not know why. Well, let's just say the speculated reasons I can think of are not good enough to end a relationship with your siblings or between a mother and her daughter who were once very close.

Keith and I were getting ready to purchase our first home together and have our first child together. Outside of this pregnancy, I brought two beautiful girls from previous relationships, named Deja and Taylor, and Keith also had a daughter whose name was Keani.

After moving into our home and finding out just a month-and-a-half later that we were expecting, you would think that we were ecstatic about all the blessings God was placing in our lives. Meanwhile, I was not fully excited for it either. Deep down, I wanted my mom and sister there to share in those moments. Over the course of the next couple months, I was able to finally reconcile with my sister, after our separation turned out to have been a result of a total misunderstanding and lack of communication. Unfortunately, circumstances were only getting worse with my mom. I just could not believe that Keith and I were experiencing in-law issues.

As time went on, just when my mother and I seemed to arrive at a crossroads of apologies and forgiveness, there would come another barrier and we would be back at square one, not speaking, and an occasionally even having a yelling match. One can only imagine how this was affecting me physically while I was pregnant...little did I know it was affecting me a lot, so much so that I maintained high blood pressure, amongst other complications throughout my pregnancy.

This stress was severely effecting my relationship with Keith. There were instances of blow-ups between the two of them just by phone that resulted in him storming out the house and not returning for several hours, no responses to texts or even my phone calls. He once expressed to me that if we lived in the same state our marriage probably wouldn't last.

A week before Thanksgiving, I had spoken with my mom and she had informed me that if I brought Keith to the family dinner at my aunt's house, she was not planning to speak or hold a conversation with him and would like the same respect. Of course I became emotional. Knowing that I was in the middle of a disagreement between my husband and mother, I did not know what to do.

212

I woke up at 4 a.m., barely being able to breathe with really bad chest pain. As I went downstairs for water, I became lightheaded and almost fell. When I went to the hospital, the doctors ran several tests and discovered with one of the blood tests that I had a blood clot. Fortunately, I was treated and sent home. However, I was instructed to stay home and told that I couldn't travel. I am not sure if this was a sign from God because of the recent information my mom had given me regarding my husband and what to expect on Thanksgiving.

The following Tuesday, we had our ultrasound and found out we were having a boy! With receiving all of the wonderful news, I was still not happy. Even though my mom and I were working on what was recently damaged, things were still not resolved between her and Keith. Over the course of several months, I had gotten calls from different individuals, giving their opinion on the drama between me, my mom, and Keith. Although our household had an abundance of blessings, I was very much missing that joy that I had longed for and not realizing that my unhappiness was causing my marriage to be unhappy.

A few weeks after Thanksgiving, I received a phone call informing me that my mother was plotting to get my oldest daughter removed from my home, as well as siding with my child's father in court. For over a year, I had been in and out of court with him. This too was an additional stress in my marriage. I remember vividly after returning home from court one day how we couldn't come to an understanding over the custody battle and being 8 months pregnant my emotions were everywhere; they were so bad that I became physical in throwing silverware. At this point I was completely confused and hurt...by everyone. I didn't understand why a mother would go to such great lengths to hurt her own child. What hurt even worse than not understanding was that there were outsiders were involved (my daughter's father). Two days after hearing this, I started having contractions and went back into the hospital. The doctors told me that if I went into labor, my son would not make it. Now, I took it upon myself to remove any negativity, drama, gossip, or anything else that was stressing me out.

Going into the new year, I felt that it was best that I not speak with my mother until after I had my son. Needless to say it did not work out that way. We spoke in the middle of January and this was the last time we spoke for several months. The conversation was anything but warming and positive. Instead, she confirmed all of the rumors that outsiders had told me. As one can imagine, I was surprised that with all of the complications thus far with my pregnancy, I didn't go into labor. One thing is for sure…receiving joy and happiness in my life seemed extremely far away.

Not too long after the final altercation with my mom, I was diagnosed with gestational diabetes. I received the diagnosis and dealt with it the best I could. Shortly after getting the news, I delivered a beautiful baby boy, although he was not born healthy.

A couple of weeks after giving birth, we noticed that Christian was sleeping more than usual, almost an entire day. We took him to the children's hospital and everything appeared fine, but we were instructed to take him for a follow-up with a cardiologist. The cardiologist had Christian on a heart monitor for a few weeks at a time, and after some testing, he decided to admit him into the hospital. Our baby was born with a heart condition and was placed on medication.

The entire time that he was in the hospital, I was there and refused to sleep. I was delirious and extremely depressed. I thought, "God, why me!? Haven't I endured enough over the past

214

couple years? When is enough, enough?" Ironically, after all we'd been through and pain that I'd felt, all I wanted was to have my mom to hold me and tell me everything was going to be okay.

The next morning, I received a phone call from my mom. God had answered my prayer, and all that had happened in the previous months was it was just a dream. Things between her and Keith remained unresolved. It was one of the worst feelings to be caught in the middle of my parent and my spouse. Entering my marriage, I honestly did not think this was going to be an issue we had to deal with.

My dad's speech often came to mind, and after I sincerely prayed over the situation and officially gave it to God, things became better. My lack of joy and happiness was not due to the absence of my mom. Instead, it came from me allowing my mom to indirectly control my marriage, not God. Everything I should have been seeking from God, I was trying to get from a person...my mother. In doing this, it caused strain on my relationship, my pregnancy, and my life as a whole. I know now what it truly means to keep God in your marriage and everyone else out. Not until I sought God completely and honestly did my marriage, my son, and life become fulfilled.

Nicole Green is a mentor and philanthropist who holds a master's degree in mechanical engineering. She is a devoted wife and mother that runs a mentoring program for teenage mothers by providing professional and positive mentors. In her spare time, she enjoys traveling, and spending time at

215

home with her family. You can find her work at www.motivatingyoungmoms.org.

This Ain't No Fairytale and Who Stole My White Picket Fence
Nieda Mathis

I remember the day like it was yesterday. Walking down the aisle on the arm of my father in my white dress, church was beautiful; husband was just as handsome as the first day we met. At the front of the church, the Pastor was waiting for me to make it down the aisle to start the ceremony. My girls were in place, looking beautiful as ever, in their fuchsia gowns and the groomsmen looked great in their steel grey tuxedos. The wedding was beautiful and amazing! When we arrived at the reception you should have seen the flowers, the decorations, and the table settings. The food was so tasty I can still taste the spices in my mouth. My day was perfect to say the least. Everything went smooth that day with the exception of me being about an hour late because Beyoncé was in town and I was stuck in traffic. None the less, my day was PERFECT!

I remember people saying that if it rained on your wedding day that signaled that there would be trouble in your marriage. When I watched the weather forecast that morning it stated chances of rain that day. I prayed and prayed for great weather and God blessed. It seemed like everything I asked for, and what I asked God to do, came to fruition. I was able to have the wedding of my dreams! I don't know how many people can actually say that. Money was flowing in my household and there were no financial restrictions on what I wanted. It seemed as if money was coming from everywhere and we were BLESSED BEYOND MEASURE. I knew that the windows of heaven had opened up and poured out a blessing just for me! So, why should I expect anything less than perfection from my marriage?

GUT CHECK! Ugh, who punched me in the stomach? What is going on? What happened? As soon as the day was over the fantasy was gone and something happened. What happened to the fairy tale life that I thought I was going to have? What happened to the white picket fence that I just knew I deserved since I had waited so long to get married? Who stole my dreams? WHAT HAPPENED? Once the wedding was over the storm began. I guess the wedding was like the calm before the storm. As soon as we said, "I DO", the enemy came with everything he had to try to make us say, "I DON'T'. I loved my husband, and I loved my marriage, and I truly believed that God had a work for us to do as soon as we got out of this storm.

One of the things that I have come to realize in this walk and being married is that some people don't tell the truth. They don't tell you the truth about marriage and ALL of the WORK it entails. Maybe my situation was different. Maybe I was just unique and had a totally different marriage than anyone else, but I felt ill equipped as a new wife.

Why didn't anyone tell me that there would be disagreements or arguments, as I call them? Why didn't they tell me that after I got married my expectations of my husband would change, even if I thought that they didn't? So many things people did not say, or I felt as if I wasn't told, but then again who would really teach me these things.

I come from a family where on the male side marriages are strong and long lasting. I have uncles that have been married for over twenty or so years, and who, in my opinion from the outside looking in, have been really good husbands to their wives. Now, if I was to survey my aunts I am SURE they would have a different story to tell. Lol! However; I have seen the women in my family struggle with marriage. I have seen them struggle to make their marriages last. I have seen long separations, divorces, and multiple marriages.

I grew up in a household where my grandfather cheated on my grandmother, had children out of wedlock, and everyone in the family knew about it. I saw him run the streets and drink. I heard him talking to other women on the phone while my grandmother was upstairs making sure the clothes were put away and that the grandchildren she was raising as her own were taken care of. I saw a woman that went to church every Sunday, served as the President of the Deaconess Board at her church for over 50 years; hold her position and title at church. My grandmother was a woman of good character who had a good heart and meant well. She was a woman who made her husband take care of his children that were born during her marriage to him; a woman, who walked with her head up, was a hard worker, classy and well put together on the outside. I saw her turn cold, heart broken, bitter, and lonely. I saw the void in her life that not many were able to see and I saw it as a young girl.

I never saw my grandparents sleep in the same bed other than vacations out of town when she was forced to sleep with him because the grandkids were taking over the other bed in a hotel room. I knew that she loved us and she showered us with so much love it was crazy; however, I never knew what real love looked like between a husband and a wife. I just knew that when I got grown and married I did not want to live like that. I did not want to hurt the way she hurt or deal with the things she dealt with. So, I fought everyday not to become the woman that raised me. How do you not become bitter when the white picket fence that you dreamed of as a child does not exist as an adult? You learn that marriages are hard work; that when you see a husband and wife that have been married for 30 plus years there is a story of their growth and the growing pains that they had to experience on their journey.

I somehow thought that those things just automatically came when you got married and that my grandparent's marriage was one in a million. That I would have smooth sailing when I got married, because I was going to make sure that I waited and married the RIGHT PERSON. What I did was place unrealistic expectations on my spouse. Could what I have seen growing up alter the way I see my husband in my marriage? Have I set standards for my husband that are unrealistic, standards that have made it hard for him to live up to and have only frustrated him as a man? Have I caused my own storm in my marriage without even realizing it? Maybe.

My mother was a teenage mother who had me at 14; she gave me to my grandparents to raise because she thought it would be in my best interest. Financially, yes. Love, yes. I had a great childhood and there are a lot of things that I would not change yet as a child I felt abandoned by my mother. As an adult I know she did what she felt was best for me, but as a child I always felt like my mother did not love me, because she gave me away. I have also experienced a lot of loss in my life. My mother passed away at the age of 44, my grandmother that raised me passed away two years after my mother, and it seemed as if all of the people who really loved me were all gone. There I was all alone.

Again, because of the things that I have dealt with in my life, have I placed unrealistic expectations on my husband and my marriage? Am I the cause for my storm?

My husband's childhood was totally different from mine. He came from parents who divorced when he was young and he lived with his father, who did not necessarily show him how to be a man. He started working at 14 to provide for himself and went into the service to make a career for himself. He had his first child at 19 and soon after he was married with 3 children and his first wife.

Now, in our marriage there have been expectations that have been put on me that he may not have realized he even had of me until after we were married. Some bad habits that were done in his first marriage were carried over into our marriage. They would argue and not talk for days, leaving room for the enemy to enter into their marriage. There are times I feel like my husband purposely does this. Knowing that we should leave no room for the enemy, I feel he will still go without talking, knowing better and the consequences of doing so, to leave room to have an excuse for certain things. If you know better you should do better, right? There are times when he picks me apart and it makes me feel less than I know God would have me to feel. We have had bouts with trust and we have had trust that was broken in the beginning of our relationship that is still yet to be repaired. Is he the cause of our storm? Is his learned behavior of what a man should be, by looking at his father's mishaps, a part of his learned behavior? Does it put unrealistic expectations on me that I may never be able to live up to? It frustrates me to no end. Does the absence of his mother at times in his life cause storms in my marriage? Her nurturing was missing and when I go to nurture my husband it's not received correctly. Does he really know how to love me as a wife and woman? Does he know how to love, due to his lack of it? Could his lack of love be the cause for the storm in my marriage?

Whatever the cause is, I am praying that we get through our storm. I want to encourage you to fight through your differences. Have open communication and always be honest with one another and respect what the other person has to say whether you agree with them or not. From the outside looking in

221

everything looks great in my marriage. From the inside out, I am fighting with everything I have inside of me to keep it together. I have gotten closer to God. I am learning to pray WITHOUT CEASING. I am learning to war for my husband and to pray for him, even when I don't feel like it and when I feel like he is in the wrong and I am the one needing prayer. I am learning to pray even when I feel like walking away and when I feel like it's becoming too hard to hold on. I am learning to pray for my husband even when I feel like he does not love or like me. I refuse to let the enemy have my marriage without the fight of his life. I have learned that you have to give God His Word back to Him and that His Word will not return back void, but must accomplish that which it was set out to do. No, I don't have the perfect marriage and No, I don't know what the outcome of my marriage will be, but what I do know is that I am a fighter. I know that I am going to war for my marriage and that the enemy can't have it. I know that God can turn things around.

So, no, I did not get the white picket fence I was hoping for. What I did get was the awakening of the warrior inside of me. I pray my story has touched you in some way. If you can relate to any of my story, I speak to the warrior inside of you and I command the warrior to arise! Fight for that which God has given you! Fight for your marriage! Fight for your husband, children, and family! What God has put together let NO man tear apart. God may have given you that husband just to grow you up and make you stronger. Know that no matter what, God will never leave you or forsake you and that ALL things, no matter what they look like, are working for your good! Continue to love God and forgive your husband if he has hurt you. Free him and yourself and turn him over to God. You cannot change him, but God, and the Word of God, can. Just be still and know that He is God. You may not have the white picket fence, but this is not the end of your story. Hold on and see what the end is going to be! To be continued...God Bless

Nieda is a true go getter in every sense of the word. Nieda is a licensed Financial Advisor and Banker and has worked over 10 years in the finance and investment industry.

Nieda has worked as a Wealth Management Advisor with Merrill Lynch and was the first African American Woman to be hired to work in the Center City Philadelphia office. While working for Merrill Lynch she also invested her time as a mentor and teacher of the stock market game. A game that teaches about stocks and investing in various inner city schools. Teaching finances and investments to children that look like her and come from the inner city where she grew up had always been a passion of hers. She was able to assist in educating children who may have never known or understood stocks, bonds, or mutual funds and open their minds to things they may have never learned without the game.

Nieda has specialized in 401k, stock options, and also seminars for women and people that want to learn about investing and want to know what their company's retirement plan has to offer them individually.

Nieda currently works as a Personal Banker with Bank of America and is an entrepreneur who runs various businesses. From Wrap Wives Philly- which is a health, nutrition, and weight management business, to Dollars and Cents Consulting, LLC which offers various aspects of financial consulting, credit and debt coaching, and financial planning.

Nieda enjoys being a wife and has been married to her husband, Phillip, since August 31, 2013. They enjoy traveling, visits to the park in the summer, and taking time with their dog, Chloe'.

They both believe in prayer and putting God first in their marriage and everything that they do as a family and individually.

Nieda' favorite scripture is Romans 8:28. "All things work together for the good of them that love God and are called according to his purpose".

Seasons
Nikita Y. Jackson

There are seasons to every marriage. At all times, you must know which season you're in and what has to be done to help you manage in that season. Most importantly, you have to know God and call on Him for who He is and ask Him to be the "spiritual prescription" you need Him to be in that season. Face the season together, learn from it, manage it together, pass the test, and move on to live a healthy, balanced life and marriage together.

IT WAS PUPPY LOVE AT FIRST SIGHT

I met my husband in grade school. It was puppy love at first sight. He was so fine. I thought this young boy walked on water. Talk about being starry-eyed. That was me. We became good friends. Where you saw one, you saw the other. Our families got used to us being inseparable. He had even gotten labeled as being "kitalized," a shortened version of my name, Nikita. We were close like this throughout high school and remained the same until we parted to pursue our futures. I headed off to college and Byron headed off to the Navy. We missed each other terribly. On his weekend leaves from the military, Byron would fly in to visit me and we'd miss each other as soon as we had to part. We decided in May 1990 we no longer could stand to be apart, so we got married. Although we continued to live separate for a while (I still had college then graduate school and he had the military) we took our vows seriously and promised one another that no matter what we'd make it. We feared the Lord way more than we feared any struggle. We understood at an early age that our families had their issues; despite being Christians and basically good people, they were not perfect. Like many families, the issues were diverse; ours included cheating, alcohol/drug abuse, and domestic violence...not all marriages lasted except for our grandparents and a few great aunts and uncles. Both our marriage role models were our grandparents. They were the matriarchs in our families. They wheeled a lot of wisdom and honor and we paid attention. We wanted what they had and we were determined to make it last. I've known Byron for 30 plus years. He has been my husband, the love of my life, soul mate, cheerleader, best friend and business partner ever since.

SEASONS

There are seasons to every marriage. At all times, you must know which season you're in and what has to be done to help you manage in that season. Most importantly, you have to know God and call on Him for who He is and ask Him to be the "spiritual prescription" you need Him to be in that season. Face the season together, learn from it, manage it together, pass the test, and move on to live a healthy, balanced life and marriage together.

Byron and I had gotten to know God personally and knew His capabilities. We walked with Him in our personal journeys, experiences, setbacks, come backs while we were in school and the navy---but never had we truly experienced Him in our marriage. We lived mostly apart the first four years of our marriage. I was wrapping up school and his Navy tour was coming to an end. When we finally settled down and lived in the same household, marriage took on a whole new meaning. We quickly learned that marriage is an institution with its own set of struggles, experiences and seasons altogether different from our personal ones because we were now one. There is a different set of rules, responsibilities and tests to pass. In order to pass the test, you must recognize the season. If you pass the test, grace will follow. So when challenges and disagreements presented themselves we managed them. They did not seem so difficult in the beginning.

TESTS AND TRIBULATIONS

We loved hard, played hard, traveled, and spent money. Our careers were flourishing. We even wrote down our vision to become owners of a catering business. We named the business and played around with menus. My husband is an excellent chef and he always, always loved making a new dish for me. While enlisted in the Navy, he picked up tons of recipes on his travels oversees. We were very happy and optimistic for our future, but small problems here and there began to surface in our marriage. I wanted to discuss and communicate about everything. He did not. We were still growing, but just not together. It seemed the moment our tests became more difficult, or we had to be more responsible to each other or make decisions about what was best for our future together, we could not turn that corner. We faced what would be a series of challenges for years to come. Communication became harder. The flesh rose up. The partnership started to fall apart. Instead of turning to God, we turned to friends. Not every friend had a personal relationship with God and so poor advice caused us to make poor decisions. I buried myself in my career and climbed higher. My husband spent more time with his boys after work. He began to drink heavily and dab in drugs. Soon he was addicted to both alcohol and drugs. His mood was changing. He disappeared often. Things around the house went missing, including money. He hid his addiction over the years. There was always some strange excuse for his behavior. The more I pressed him, the more he would get angry and behave erratically. Eventually things got to a point where he could no longer hide his addiction and we could not ignore the trouble we were in. Over the next seven years, Byron had checked into half a dozen rehab facilities from Florida to Maine. He stayed clean on and off but nothing seemed to stick. In fact, his addiction had gotten worse. We went back to our roots-the church. We attended regularly and got involved with the marriage ministry. Although we attended church, so did the devil. The marriage ministry forced us to face some of our demons. Privately we began to address our problems with communication, as it was our source of failures. We read Scripture and concentrated on 1 John 4:19. We spent more time on the love of God; understanding how much He truly loved us with no strings attached and how much grace He gives us freely without deserving it. We figured out that this is the same love and grace we must have with one another. We grew some. We meditated on this truth about the love of God. This truth also meant we were commanded to love ourselves. If we love ourselves as God loves us, we can love one another unconditionally. And through that love, comes grace and mercy. Not condemnation, or guilt. It appeared we were figuring it out. We had gotten back to why we loved each and what drew us to one another in the first place. The ministry had added value to our lives. We had finally turned a corner and did not realize. We had also just touched the surface of some deeply rooted issues my husband had that neither one of us realized. That addiction demon was still lurking and was building its own case in my husband's head and ultimately in our marriage as to why accepting the love of God and the love of ourselves was not plausible. While I moved forward with knowing that the unconditional love of God saves us by any means necessary, and that there is no way I could ever be loss to God, Byron could not wrap his heart and head around this belief. He felt guilty and condemned because of his addiction. He could not forgive himself and could not believe that God could either. Besides, this love as described in 1 John 4:19 looked nothing like what he saw in the marriage of his father and mother or a few close family members. Nevertheless, we kept trying to get through this problem, seeking the Word of God, staying in fellowship, staying connected with ministry, believing in scripture, seeking counseling and focusing on Deuteronomy 7:7-8 trying desperately to live under the grace of God.

I'M NOT YOUR BEARD ANYMORE

A few more years had passed. We had two small children. We had great moments and some not so great. So much suffering and affliction had come upon us that our existence was threatened. I felt alone. I wanted to give up. I was tired. I figured, I'm a career woman. I got it going on. My mind was telling me that I could take care of my two children. Go ahead; get out of your marriage. It is no longer working. He's not trying hard enough. God does not want the children and me to live this way. We've lost so much, cars, a home, money, and jewelry. You name it, it was all taken away. The addiction was horrible. What did love have to do with all of this anyway? One day the Lord spoke to me and said, " Seek me with all your heart. I never left you. Did I not command you to love? I was ashamed and convicted. I allowed my frustration and fear to overtake my faith in God. I repented and earnestly asked God's forgiveness. I needed a fresh anointing --- a do over. The scales fell away from my eyes and I realized I had the power to intercede for my husband, marriage, my children and my family. I recognized my season. It was time to fight. I recognized the grace that empowers. As believers, we have spiritual authority over our situations ----Authority in Jesus name and the blood of the cross. We have authority over powers and principalities and

229

darkness. When we have a divine assignment from God; Angels of God are sent to defend us as we press through our assignment—our test.

A few days had passed since my revelation and I was reading through Genesis about the first partnership—Adam and Eve. I remember thinking how this couple failed to recognize the season they were in because like my husband and I, they too were caught up in all the good stuff; no worries and no clue how to handle a relational tribulation. I dozed off to sleep and the Holy Spirit spoke to me and said, " Move out of my way. Only I can save your husband. You must be willing to let go and believe in me. You must know he has to believe who I am for himself. He has to truly understand the depth of my love for him. He has to know me by my names. Everything you both need I AM."

I woke around 3:00am. My husband was downstairs working. I could smell the onions and other seasonings as he was preparing for a catering event. I walked into the kitchen and said, "honey, if you mess up again I will leave you. In other words, if you give into your addiction, I'm not going to stick around. The kids and I won't have a choice. I proceeded to say, only God knows why, 'drive me to the train station and I'll get to work from there. I get off at 3:00pm. Pick me up and together we'll pick up the kids from school." Everything in me was panicking. We only had the one car and I just gave it away. My inner voice was screaming, what are you doing? You have not trusted him alone with the vehicle in a long time. It's the only transportation you have…to work, to school, to church, to everywhere and you just gave it away! Yet I trusted the Holy Spirit. The thing is, I knew my life was going to change in less than 24 hours. I knew it in the depths of my soul. I understood I was entering into a new season and I was going solo. In short, after my husband worked his catering event, he disappeared. My husband did not show up to meet me at the train station. I called my girlfriend that worked the catering event with him. She said the event went well and she assumed Byron had left to head home. After all, the event only required them to set-up. I proceeded to ask my friend if she would mind picking me up from the train station and then pick up the boys from school. I explained everything to her about what was going on with Byron and I. I made up in my mind that I was no longer going to act as his beard. The mask was coming off so the real healing could begin. I was so angry and so sick and tired of living an unpredictable life. His behavior was sporadic. I absolutely hated living like this. I had momentarily loss all rationale. I was willing to walk away from my marriage, the vehicle he'd taken, everything. The wear and tear on the children had reached its tipping point. My oldest son just could not take it anymore. He had emotionally checked out. He was only 11 years old. Looking at his face when I arrived to his school in another person's car was enough for me to finally move out of the way. He already knew daddy had gone out again.

My girlfriend reached out to her husband and shared what happened with her husband. Her husband called me and said sis, you can be angry, but be smart. Don't walk away from the car. You need it. Call the police and report it stolen. Explain why. I did as I was told. You see, God always has a ram in the bush. He sent me a gatekeeper through my girlfriend and her husband to instruct me. This man too had experienced a relationship with someone who had a drug addiction. It was the mother of his first child. He knew all too well the impact of this addiction and was able to help me see clearly when things got really bad. Unknowingly to any of us, this couple had been placed in my life to play a significant role in saving my marriage.

I got the kids settled and then called the police. An officer came to the house and took down my information and called it in. Within the hour the officer returned. He found the car and my husband. Unfortunately, for my husband when the officer did a background check, the officer discovered my husband had a warrant for his arrest. The reason. My husband failed to show up to court in another state for an unpaid parking ticket. The officer explained to me that my husband had been arrested and was going to jail until the matter could be resolved. I refused to pay the bail. I was going to be obedient to the words God had spoken to me. I was going to trust Him. That unpaid parking ticket saved my husband's life and ultimately our family. As a result of me not paying the bail, my husband was jailed for almost a year before he was released. That was Spring 2008. It would be three years and several shelters and halfway houses later before my husband and I would ever truly communicate again.

WE GET A DO OVER

"My grace is sufficient for you." God is able to make all grace abound to you, so that having all sufficiency in all things and all times, you may abound" every good work." -II Corinthians 2:8.

We get "grace to help in time of need, (Hebrews 4:16) and when you have suffered a little while, the God of all grace will himself restore, confirm, strengthen and establish you." -I Peter 1:10)

These scriptures echoed in my heart, mind and soul for three years as I patiently trusted and believed that God would do just what he said. I was obedient to God and moved out of the way so that He could deal with my husband and deal with me. What I had not realized was that God had already planned our destiny.

232

We just had to do our part and trust Him. I believed in His promises to me.

During my separation from my husband, I buried all my energies and extra time into the church with the boys in tow. I had to stay alive and stay productive for the boys and for myself. I was devoted to God as he filled me with a fresh anointing every day. The church became the boys and me second home. Members became part of our extended family and we were theirs too. I couldn't have made it, any other way. I was learning the character of God. I was being discipled and stretched. I was happy. The boys were happy. We were at peace and thriving once more. I allowed Him to have His way in my life. I had gotten completely out of the way. Whatever was next, I would be ready.

I would discover months later from Byron, that 11-11-11 was his official sobriety date. God had taken away my husband's desire to ever pick up and use again. And that on Christmas Sunday December 2011, he got over his fear showed up to my safe-haven. He walked right down the aisle of our church home and took a seat near the front row. I'll never forget that day because I was giving the church announcements as I watched in disbelief, this man who appeared to have a new walk and a brighter outer image. God had made his move. A new season was dawning. I had to decide what I needed from God to manage it. In this season, God said, "be still and actively wait for my instruction. Hear me." And I did. I did not run to my husband. I watched him. I observed him. I learned the new him. I listened to his words when he spoke to the children, members of our church family and me. I gave attention to every detail about him. What I interpreted from all this watching…the word Grace. Grace is the love of God shown to the unlovely, the restless, and the unmerited favor of God. – J. Gresham McChen.

233

My husband was changing. He was fighting for his very existence, for his family and for his marriage. I never doubted he loved the boys and me. He just lost his way. He had to go through his very own personal season to be the man God designed him to be: The head of our household. Our strong tower and leader. My king and go to person. I had to be actively patient and wait for God to finish the work He had started. Another year had passed as we worked on our friendship. The children had cautiously accepted him back into their lives.

They missed him dearly, but slow to show it all at once. I missed him, my friend and partner. We eventually dated. It was love all over again. Not puppy love. The real thing. I was starry eyed. Through God I was able to love my husband better than before. Though I never stopped truly loving him, or praying for him, I was able to let the ice around my heart melt and forgive. He was wiser, stronger, better. We communicated more than ever. We unpacked the past hurts, disappointments, and failures and buried them, never to revisit them again. In 2013, we were one once more. We prepared for the new season with fresh eyes concerning our marriage and family. We revisited our future business plans to become entrepreneurs. Our names are victor and victory. We are more than conquerors. We are passing the test. We are winning again. Our catering business is growing and doing well. Our oldest son is now in his sophomore year of college. The youngest son is an honors student in middle school. Our marriage is better than before. We keep God first and heed His calling. Byron counsels others faithfully on substance abuse. He tells his story often, unafraid and unashamed. He is employed with the government and works full-time. It has been a long road to recovery for not just my husband, but for our entire family. Our transformation was a very public one. Our marriage evolved in front of family, church members, friends, co-workers. There was no hiding everything. As I said before, we were inseparable. Where you saw one, you saw the other. There was no mistaken when the other half was missing, something was not right. Thank God for Jesus. Whoever calls on the name of God shall be saved. In every season I recognized what I needed him to be in our marriage and for me when I had to step up and play the many positions as a "single-married woman" with two young boys, I called on Him a great deal. Jehovah Jireh-He was my provider. Jehovah Shalom-He was my Peace. Jehovah-Raah-He was my Shepherd. Jehovah Rapha-He was my healer. Jehovah Shammah-He was always there for me.

I'd like to akin myself to Ruth in the bible. She was loyal, obedient and loved God. She was a true Ephesians 5:22-24 woman.

Wives should put her husband first, as she does the Lord. A husband is the head of his wife, as Christ is the head and the Savior of the church, which is his own body. Wives should always put their husbands first, as the church puts Christ first.

Marriage is an institution that thrives on God, love, honor and commitment. It has seasons you must adapt to. It is beautiful and at times it can be difficult, but through God all things are possible. Face your seasons together, learn from them, manage them together, pass the test, and move on to live a healthy, balanced life and marriage together. God redeems. God heals. God restores. God loves unconditionally. His grace is sufficient.

Nikita Y. Jackson is an entrepreneur and has over 20 years of leadership experience in nonprofit management. She has utilized her educational and work experience to provide technical assistance to support organizations large and small in meeting their highest level of achievement in grant writing, board development, strategic planning, and program evaluation.

As an entrepreneur, Nikita is co-business owner of Brandon's Culinary Art Catering with her husband, Chef Byron. Brandon's catering offers a wide variety of distinctive cuisine and unparalleled service to meet their customers social, personal, and business needs. In 1991, Nikita received her B.A. in Mass Communications and Urban Planning from Dillard University in New Orleans, LA and in 1992 earned her M.S. through an accelerated program from the New School for Social Research, Graduate School of Management and Urban Policy in New York City. She received a Leadership Certificate in Nonprofit Management from the University of Delaware Professional Management Program in 2013.

Nikita married the love of her life on May 7, 1990 and they have two children. Her life verse is "Above all, love each other deeply, because love covers over a multitude of sins."- 1 Peter 4:8

Until
Death
Do You
Part

A Word From
E. Lynn Reed

"But if serving the LORD seems undesirable to you, then choose for yourselves this day whom you will serve...But as for me and my household, we will serve he LORD." - Joshua 24:15a,e

This verse heralds the resounding resolve of committed Christian women throughout the world. *Wives on Fire* is no exception. Statistics show that convictional Christian couples, couples who attend church together and are committed to walking with The Lord, don't divorce much at all. The 50% divorce rate does not apply to these couples. The testimonies in *Wives on Fire* will certainly help to bring encouragement and comfort to many women who may be facing difficulties in their marriage while also making us aware of alternative possibilities. Successful marriages still exist! It may look bad from where you are but "...a cord of three strands is not quickly broken."

Blessings!

A Word From
Marsha Redd

So often, we as wives perceive the trials and tribulations in our lives as experiences that are unique unto us. We tell ourselves that no one else has endured the types of pains and frustrations that we have. As someone who has coached wives for the past 17 years, I have learned that there's power and healing in community. Wives need other wives that they can relate to. They need exposure to wives who can affirm that they are not alone, and that there's hope for a brighter tomorrow. *Wives on Fire* meets this critical need head on.

Wives on Fire is a must read for both wives and soon-to-be wives. This book will bring you comfort, lighten your spirit, and provide hope and encouragement to stay the course. Moreover, this book will empower you to empower others who are struggling in their marriage. The journey of over 30 wives is shared in an incredibly candid and compelling manner. The book highlights the leading of the Holy Spirit and the Word of God as catalysts of healing in the lives of wives. The tragedies and triumphs shared in this book are remarkable. And at the center, is a collective commonality of faith in the Lord Jesus Christ.

I'm excited about all the lives that will be touched through *Wives on Fire*, and I'm especially excited about all the marriages that will be saved.

Intimacy and Grief
Shanna M. Williams

I stared out the window contemplating how I could leave my husband. A tentative plan was to cut and dye my hair, change my name, and pay cash for a one-way bus ticket out of town. I desperately felt like I needed to leave him, everyone in my life, and the pain behind me. Maybe I would go to the west coast or to another country, perhaps? My plans were far from concrete, but regularly played themselves out as a fantasy in my mind. I had a strong desire to leave everyone and every memory of the tragedy that had befallen our marriage behind me.

When my husband and I first fell in love and got married, we knew we needed support to avoid the pitfalls we had seen in other marriages in our family. Through our church and various marriage workshops, we learned that God's design for intimacy involved fullness of emotional, spiritual, and physical intimacy. My husband, being the sweet and kind man that he is, eagerly attended every workshop with me and we openly discussed how we would apply the principles we learned to keep intimacy alive in our marriage. Because we were so committed to this goal, we felt we would have a stress free, loving marriage and the flames of intimacy would never burn out.

We were ecstatic when we found out I was pregnant with our first child. We happily shared our news with everyone, with the doctors commending me on how healthy I and the baby were and how supportive my husband was. He attended every appointment with me and communicated openly with the doctors. Sadly, he was also right beside me when it was revealed in an ultrasound

243

that, for some unknown reason, our baby had unexpectedly died in utero. Shocked and heartbroken, I burst into tears. My husband held me and we cried together trying to figure out how to piece our lives back together. I went into a grief stricken shell and my husband had to take over from that point. He and the doctors made the decision for me to give birth to our baby in the hospital the next day. He also coordinated with a funeral home to plan a small service for our baby boy, who we named Christian. I went through the motions and found only brief solace in being able to hold and kiss our son's lifeless body, before they took him from my arms to the hospital morgue.

Soon after the funeral, our loved ones, who had offered us comfort and condolences at the time of our loss, went back to their daily routines. Some passively or non-verbally let me know I needed to "move on." But my world had stopped and heart was still freshly broken. I was merely a shell of a person in my marriage. My husband grieved as well, but had to take over the needs of the household, while I curled up in bed and cried. Our emotional communication suffered, as I only felt able to focus on losing Christian. When my husband tried to discuss plans for the future, I became inconsolable. Fear gripped his heart and he watched over me day and night, because I openly told him that I felt as if I no longer had a reason to live. Spiritually, I felt disconnected from God. I knew God loved me, but why did He let our baby die? My husband prayed over and for me, but I wasn't able to pray and struggled with thoughts of returning to church. Physically, my husband's touch brought me to tears. Sex prior to this point had been an exciting way to conceive a baby, so now every time we were intimate it triggered raw emotional pain. My breasts were painful and engorged with milk for a baby I would never nurse. If my husband touched them or my stomach which was still stretched from our son, I withdrew. Sometimes because I wanted to feel loved I would request sex, only to further confuse my husband by crying myself to sleep or verbally contemplating suicide afterwards.

At some point, I made the decision that I wanted to guarantee a trip to Heaven to be with my baby; I wasn't sure that suicide would grant me this option. Soon, I began to have fantasies about leaving my husband and everything behind. I even casually searched the internet to learn how others had managed to "disappear" without a trace. Thoughts of starting over with a new life gave me relief from my internal turmoil. I told myself that I had failed my husband and my family. I even questioned my sense of identity as a woman. I felt a great amount of shame over my loss and couldn't deal with the insensitivity of others or the constant reminders of my baby, whose urn I lovingly cradled every night.

What saved our marriage and brought intimacy back to the forefront? To put it simply, God did. My husband didn't yet know my runaway fantasy. So I was shocked one night when he held me close and cried out, "Don't leave me!" God allowed me to get past my own grief and see what my spouse was really saying to me. These words meant that emotionally, he missed me and wanted to reconnect. These words meant spiritually he wanted his prayer partner back. And physically, he was telling me that he feared I would end my life, or at least disappear from his. God spoke to my heart and reminded me that the baby I loved so much...was the spitting image of my husband. I sadly imagined my son looking down from heaven and feeling as if he had ruined our lives. That thought made me realize that, although my child was gone, I was still a mother and wife. That night, I immediately promised my husband I would never leave him. That no matter what, we would come through this trial, and our marriage would become better, not bitter.

We returned to our church's marriage ministry and gathered information on how to grow our marriage through this storm. God worked through other Christian couples, who would share with us that they too had lost a child. They shared with us how they had either saved their marriage or what they wished they had done differently to prevent the end of their marriage. We joined support groups for parents of a child who had died and learned that our feelings and the issues in our marriage were normal; however, we knew with God, our problems were not insurmountable. We could overcome, and there would be life for our marriage again. Slowly, we began to talk about the future again. We began to worship regularly, study the Bible, and pray together. We began to openly discuss our fears and sadness with one another, working to become emotionally "naked and unashamed". With our emotional and physical intimacy rebuilding, our physical intimacy soon flourished again. God has since allowed us to share our testimony with other couples. My husband and I have been blessed to support other couples through various marital trials, and frequently God leads us to other couples dealing with the loss of their child. With God's grace, our marital intimacy was shaken, but not easily broken. The scripture that gave us strength as we walked this journey to rebuild our marital intimacy in the face of grief was Zechariah 13:9, "This third I will put into the fire: I will refine them like silver and test them like gold. They will call on my name and I will answer them. I will say, 'these are my people' and they will say 'the Lord is our God.'"

Shanna M. Williams, LCSW, MEd is a licensed clinical social worker and educator residing in the Greater Philadelphia area. She and her husband, William, have been together for 6 years, and happily married since 2011.

After the loss of their first child, she and her husband fully dedicated their marriage to Christ. God has led them to focus on learning and teaching His plan for building a Christian marriage that is equipped to manage the storms of life. Shanna supports her husband in his role as Assistant Servant leader of Enon Tabernacle Baptist Church's "Not Easily Broken" marital enrichment ministry in Philadelphia, PA. She also serves as a Christian Counselor with Enon's Balm of Gilead Counseling Ministry. Professionally, Shanna has over 15 years of experience as a psychotherapist and educator of sexual health and intimacy, family therapy, and marital issues.

Shanna is a professional member of the American Association of Sexuality Educators, Counselors, and Therapists and the National American Association of Christian Social Workers. She is currently pursuing her Certificate of Biblical Studies at Palmer Seminary in Pennsylvania.

Shanna's passion is providing spiritually centered support to wives and couples. Her guiding wife verse is Proverbs 31:26 - "She opens her mouth with wisdom; and in her tongue is the law of kindness".

What About the Children?
Stacy Harrison

I came from an awesome family. It was a household of three girls, with a mom and dad that showed love on a regular basis. We lived in a nice neighborhood and always had the latest cars. We took regular trips and we loved to shop. Life was great! There was only one problem...it seemed like whenever there was a full moon; my dad would abuse my mom. It seemed like he would always start an argument pertaining to something I did. Why is her dress dirty? Why does she have toys in the living room? Now, don't get me wrong, my mom would fight back every time. This abuse started from the age of two until I was 13. My mom finally decided to part ways and never looked back.

My mom had us going to church at a young age. At the age of 13, I gave my life to Christ. I went to church faithfully looking for answers from God concerning my parents. I was living between two households and thinking it was my fault they had broken up. But most of all, I went to church asking God to help me with the consistent dreams I had of the abuse I seen for many years and praying I didn't go to jail for killing my husband if he ever hit me. For years, I clearly visualized myself in an orange jumpsuit behind prison walls. I wanted to be delivered from this nightmare for what seemed like centuries.

When I started dating, I constantly had my guard up, protecting my heart. My questions would be: Why do you like me? What do you want from me? You see, my mom had taught me how to make money and how to hold my own, but not how to share my heart and love someone else. I dated some awesome young men, but the first thing I would say is don't fall in love with me and don't say "I love you." Whenever I felt a guy falling for me, I would break it off. I never wanted to deal with the drama, arguing, and most of all, the fighting.

I never had a fight with a guy, but I was always ready to. Years later, I did finally meet the man of my dreams, or so I thought. We got married and had a child. The relationship for me was great as long as he had his money and I had mine. He paid his bills and I paid mine and gave him my portion of the household bills. He wasn't very affectionate, so that worked well with me. We lasted for about five years, and finally I had enough. I packed up and moved out. You see, the relationship was competitive and I felt like we were never on the same team. I was looking for so much more in a man, but not really sure what that was.

I moved to a new town and relocated to a new church. I joined the singles ministry and was taught to start getting in tune with myself. I learned to focus on me and learned to forgive, even when I thought it wasn't my fault. I decided to go to counseling and prepare myself for the next man God would send my way one day.

The first appointment with the counselor was just to get acquainted with each other and to discuss my outcomes once I was done with our sessions. At the second appointment, she asked a few questions, but the one question that really got me was "Tell me about your childhood." I lost it! That took me all the way back to my parents' issues. I realized that I was holding on to the baggage from my childhood that had caused me to avoid sharing my heart with anyone without expecting disappointment.

Once we made that discovery, she started taking a healing approach with me. I cried for months, praying and thinking I was over these issues just to find out I never dealt with it fully. I had just camouflaged it for many, many years. I continued counseling for a few more sessions and was very appreciative of the outcome. It gave me a lot of clarity on so many issues. I was ever so grateful for her assistance. My life was never the same again.

Once I got over the pain of my past, I started calling people from my past and apologizing for all the hurt I had caused them. My biggest relief came from calling my ex-husband and apologizing for all that I did wrong in our relationship. Although he had his fair share of blame, I didn't expect an apology from him. I wanted to be FREE from everything and just to be in God's perfect will. It wasn't just about having a new man. I didn't want to block any blessings God had in store for me.

Three years later, God sent my king when I least expected it. I didn't realize it at first. It took me a while to figure it out. He's everything my mother and my pastor told me to find in a man. I didn't feel comfortable for a while, just sitting back and waiting for him to mess up and do or say something stupid so I could determine that he was just like everyone else. I had my guard up, but he kept coming on stronger and stronger. I finally broke down and explained to him my past during a heated argument over my negative comments and actions.

It's been 16 years and I love him more today than I did yesterday. He taught me how to love by his overwhelming expression of love. We've learned to communicate and how to agree to disagree. He's the calm and rational side of me. When they say that opposites attract, I truly agree. We have built a bond over 16 years of marriage that can't be broken with God on our side.

Please understand that your actions, good or bad, around your children can cause a lifetime of effects. When I discussed a situation with my mother, she told me I was only two years old when it occurred. Remember, not every child will handle life situations as I did. There will be children that will grow up and expect the same abuse that they saw their parents go through and think that's how life is because their parents did it. Some will become that abuser and take matters to another level. This can become deadly. If you have been in an abusive relationship, please seek help for yourself and your children. Please know that abuse is not love! It is the sign of a weak-minded person with issues. You can do nothing to help an abuser but leave and pray for him from afar. When is enough, enough? Will you be the one with the sunglasses on a rainy day, saying that your migraine is acting up again?

God is your source! Seek God for direction and trust His Word to be true. He loves you and His Word will never turn void. Trust God to send you your soul mate. He's faithful and able! Get your life in order so that you will be ready when he comes. Clean your house, get your credit right, and work on your savings accounts and more. God knows what you need, but sometimes He's waiting on you to be ready.

Whatever relationship you enter, think about what you want to be best for you and your children that you have or plan to have one day.

The wife in the Bible I compare myself to now would be Sarah. Hebrew 11:1 "Now faith is the substance of things hoped for, the evidence of things not seen."

Stacy Harrison married her awesome husband, Clinton, on September 4, 1999. Together the two love sharing with others the true example of how blended families do work! She is a proud mother of three children and one grandson.

Stacy gave her life to Christ at the early age of 13. At the age of 16 thru 40, she taught Sunday school. Stacy always has a passion for reaching out to the youth. During her last 10 years of teaching Sunday school, she became the Assistant to the youth minister at Alpha Worship Center in Bear, DE. Stacy is currently a member of Seeds of Greatness in New Castle, Delaware under the leadership of Jerome L. Lewis Sr.

Stacy has worked in the mortgage industry for 30 years. She has a strong passion to assist others with the American dreams of homeownership. She has a desire to assist families out of debt. She is a qualified result driven sales professional with more than 30 years of experience in business development, Mortgage financing, and financial literacy. She demonstrates the ability to establish and maintain productive relationships with existing and potential clients and contacts. She poses strong leadership skills with the demonstrated ability to train and mentor teams to success. She has excellent communication and presentation skills to include direct interaction with a diverse internal and external population.

~Her Wife Verse~

"I have chosen the way of truth and faithfulness; Your ordinances have I set before me" Psalms 119:30

Trusting God In More Intimate Ways
Dr. Tonia Conley

Genesis chapter 29 describes a young woman with "tender eyes." The daughter of a prominent family, she was abandoned and rejected by the two men who should have protected her. Tricked into a marital situation, she lived her life united to a husband who craved to be with someone else. After a short period of wedded bliss, she was forced to accept the ugly truth...she knew she was unloved by her husband. Her self-esteem, confidence and security evaporated, and she grieved daily. She was unseen and unwanted by her husband. Everything about her was devalued. In spite of man's rejection, her heavenly Father saw her value and the heard the secret longings of her heart.

A modern-day Leah, I too was tricked into marriage, not by external forces, but internal determinations, laced with naivety. "Surely he loved me! Why wouldn't he?" Sure, I had heard about his reputation. At times, my anxiety was so strong it was palatable.

It was the December 23rd, 1998, and by all indications, I was doing well. I was a professional woman, holding an advanced degree, having bought and built my first home at age 29, and a single parent; although not by choice, but by force. By the world's standards, I had it going on!

But on the inside was a tremendous void, a void that kept me in free-falling mode. It was a void I had not anticipated, nor welcomed. It was an unexplainable void that allowed me to function by day with a smile, while crumpling at night in despair. At my mother's urging, I attended her annual Christmas holiday gala, where friends old and new get together, catch up on old times, and share their intended plans for the future. It's where you learn about the newly engaged, anticipated wedding dates, and the pregnancies of friends and family. I wanted no part of it. Christmas, my favorite holiday, was tainted with the reality of separation and divorce. Contaminated with emotional pangs of a broken heart, I accepted it, but didn't understand it.

I understood the finality of divorce, but I just couldn't wrap my understanding around why this was now my new reality. Why? I was the young minister, committed to God's Word, focused on ministry and family. Why? I had been a good wife. Why was I being forced to live this reality I didn't ask for or understand? Wrestling with this mindset daily, needless to say, I had no interest in attending the annual event. I guess "Christmas just ain't Christmas without the one you love!" My mother begged me to come, and other family members who came into town for the party pleaded. I relented and went. I was clear, though, that I would only show up in time to clean up for my parents.

I showed up in jeans and a sweatshirt, totally out of dress and character for a celebration. I even wore my most celebratory mask for the guests. I greeted everyone with a warm embrace and "holy kiss." I was greeting them with a sincere heart, while hiding genuine pain. As I made my rounds to each guest, there he was, a stranger in the midst of all the familiar faces. Then I remembered that he was the stranger who had received a special invitation, another stark reminder of why I should have stayed home.

My uncle and his wife had invited him. I remembered hearing something about it a few weeks in advance of the party. I remembered that he was coming to my parents' party at their home to meet my cousin, who would be driving in from 8 hours away with her parents. When greeting everyone, I came face-to-face with him. I said, "Well, since you are a guest in my mother's house, you can have a holiday hug, too." Internally, I was screaming at the top of my lungs, "WHAT? They invited him here to meet her, and l live here? No way. I must be worse off than the late night void let on."

The intensity of my low self-esteem coupled with the audacity of family bringing a stranger to meet my cousin, to play matchmaker for two people who were living nearly 500 miles apart. And to do it at my mother's house...they must have been looking at the same things my former husband was looking at. I guess I just didn't fit the bill for them, either. No wonder my ex had walked off with a 72-hour notice.

One day, we were a normal family of three (mother, father, and daughter), preparing to move to a townhome apartment. The next thing I knew, the earth stopped rotating and someone pulled the carpet from under my feet and I was free falling into desperation. He made his pronouncement: "When we move on Thursday, I'm not moving with you," he said.

"Huh? What are you talking about? We are moving because you wanted to!" It was as if he was speaking a foreign language. I couldn't understand it, let alone process what he was saying. Pushing understanding and processing aside, within 72 hours, my world changed and I was clueless. In the famous words of Alice on the '70s sitcom, "What just happened here?" I couldn't make sense of it. I begged and pleaded, but he walked away, leaving me alone and lonely. I was alone to pay the bills, alone with my thoughts, alone in our bed, alone to care for our daughter. ALONE! But why? I even had to learn how to compartmentalize my emotions and stuff down my feelings. No matter how often I asked, he couldn't offer me an answer. He would only say, "I don't want to be married to you anymore!"

The anger, frustration, and disappointment were overwhelming. All three rolled in to my room like a thunderous cloud each evening, as if they were on a scheduled time clock. Crying all night in a fetal position was embarrassing. Having to figure out how to navigate my life in this "new reality" made me feel like a foreigner in my own world. I was frustrated because I could no longer make sense of my life. I wasn't sure how, when, or why I was here. I just knew that I didn't want to be! I hated being here.

Eventually, I stopped begging, stopped asking why, and turned off the porch light. I settled in to my reality. I was disappointed because I thought this was forever. Forever was gone and I had to bury my dreams because life ran out of the marriage. I had to bury the dreams in the cemetery of my heart and mind. Obviously, there would be no reason to dig up the dead.

One day, I realized my anger, frustrations, and disappointments were about God. I was mad...really mad. As far as I was concerned, God had let this happen to me. My father died by choice, and now my husband was also gone. I was abandoned by the two men who were supposed to love and protect me. Both left me exposed and vulnerable. So I quickly surmised that the only way to navigate the world would be through self –preservation. Simply stated, I would put up the walls and guard my life all by myself!

So when a chance meeting turned into a life-long love affair, I was excited that God had sent me a husband. God heard the desires of my heart. But secretly, I was terrified. Yeah, I heard God. He announced this handsome stranger as "my husband and my covering." I politely declined. "I've already had one of those. No thanks!"

Gentle in his approach and extremely patiently, the handsome, godly stranger pursued me with God's grace, allowing me to ebb and flow. Torn between my heart's desire and my harsh reality, the year-and-a-half courtship was a refreshing walk into marriage. There were discussions and conversations about everything, even pre-marital counseling. Everything seemed just fine. But like with anything else in life, it's always calm before the storm. Ten days after the nuptials and absolutely beautiful wedding ceremony... KABOOM!

Suddenly, there was one long argument. It never ended. I dare say it persisted for years. I was MISERABLE! It was the same issue with various topics. I was so wounded and so angry from the past that I couldn't speak to the issues or hear God's voice. I definitely couldn't lower the walls of self-preservation I had built. We were fighting about everything. You name it and it was argued about. It was all too much to process. I wanted out and wanted it now! Obviously, marriage wasn't for me. I felt unlovable and the negatives of the past were setting up shop in my present, trying to determine my future. There seemed to be no end in sight. The confusion was so great that I didn't hear God's voice for several years. The stress of a new marriage, residue of anger from a dead marriage, and my struggle to trust the handsome stranger-turned-husband was deafening. I asked myself countless times, "Where is God and why isn't He talking to me?"

In reality, I prayed often and believed God, but I had dropped my expectations of God. Subconsciously, I was accepting defeat, and I consciously acted upon it. The reality was that I was not believing or trusting God for anything. Then one day, I heard a message that challenged me to know Him

259

differently...intimately. So I reached for God, asking Him to show himself to me on another level, inviting Him into a secret place which was padlocked with hurt and disappointment; preventing escape from anger, frustrations, distrust, and contempt. They were like termites eating away at my self-esteem, and marriage, from behind-the-scenes.

Enough was enough. I cried out to God asking Him to reveal Himself to me in intimate ways. After a three-year hiatus, God spoke to me directly. I heard it in my brokenness. He said, "Trust me! You are what victory looks like." Suddenly, I was reminded of previous victories, reminded that God handpicked the handsome stranger just for me. Although there were challenges and I wanted to run and hide, God's voice gave me tranquility I had never known. The tide changed. I no longer looked at the stranger-turned-husband for protection, peace, and to build me. Instead, I trusted God for that and more.

The most ironic thing was that I had spent years blaming my first husband for not being perfect and my best husband for the crimes of the first. Being emotionally homeless, physically abandoned, and feeling outcast was the trifecta that caused me to drag the corpse (the embodiment of a harsh past) with me. When I cut loose the corpse, I could see the horizon. From the cleft of the rock, I saw God moving in so many areas of my life. So I took my victory lap by passing the baton to God.

Marriage requires 100% from the husband as well as the wife. There are seasons when the distribution is skewed. As a second-time wife, I see the importance of integrity between me and God. Vulnerable submission to the Lord is key; offering God my hidden self allows Him to cleanse me and rain His spirit on me.

To the woman who reads this...

I pray that you reach for a victorious marriage, knowing that a victorious marriage is based upon honesty with self, God, and spouse. We can never predict or control the actions of another, not even a husband. However, genuine vulnerability with God positions each of us for greatness and offers residual greatness for everyone and everything we are connected to. My victory happened when I began trusting God in more intimate ways.

A wife's recipe for a victorious marriage has only five ingredients needed:

Remember you are fearfully and wonderfully made in God's image;

Learn God's timing and vocabulary (operate God's way);

Be emotionally honest with self, God, and husband;

Forgive those who have wronged you (accidently and purposely);

Put your all on the altar of God (be submissive to God's will).

Blessings on you!

 Rev. Dr. Perry Conley is a native Delawarean from New Castle County. A graduate of Spelman College (1989) in Atlanta, GA, with a Bachelor of Arts in Psychology, a Masters of Arts in Theology & Counseling from Palmer Seminary (1996) in Philadelphia, PA, and an earned doctorate in Administration & Educational Leadership from Delaware State University, Dover, DE (2011).

Licensed for ministry in August 1990 at the 8th Street Baptist Church, she realized the "Call-to-be-an-Instrument" in God's Hand at an early age. She was ordained in April 2007 at the

Metropolitan Baptist Church, Philadelphia, PA, where she served as the Pastor of the INSPIRED Youth Ministry. Affirmed an Elder (2012), Tonia faithfully serves the Resurrection Center fellowship as assistant to the chancellor of the Levitical order. Her ministerial experiences include but are not limited to: volunteer chaplain at Lankenau Hospital (PA), and Christiana Care (DE), Saddleback Leadership training, youth minister, annual recognition days, Youth Ministry Leadership Conferences, Women's Conferences, ministry counseling (family, marriage, youth), New Testament instructor (Union Seminary @ Mt. Pleasant Baptist Church), and numerous opportunities to minister the Word of God in houses of *praise and worship* throughout the east-coast.

Dr. Conley is a former employee of Delaware State University, where she served as Director of the Ronald E. McNair Post-Baccalaureate Achievement Program; Educational Program Coordinator with the Upward Bound Program of Delaware Technical Community College; and Executive Director of the William 'Hicks' Anderson Community Center. Most recently, God has *elevated* her to serve as the Campus and Academic Affairs Director with the University of Phoenix. Her chosen career path provides the opportunity to exercise her commitment to God's call, and her passion for working with teens and young adults, throughout the community.

Rev. Conley currently attends the Resurrection Center with her husband, Wydell Conley, and two daughters, Hillari-Cordelia, and Aryelle-Whitney; under the spiritual guidance of Dr. S. Todd Townsend, Bishop. Tonia shares the "Good News" and walks by faith daily; seeking God's anointed direction for her life.

Journey to My Purpose
Valerie Stancill

What kind of Thanksgiving is this?

In 2000, my husband, Benny, was scheduled for a stress test due to changes found on his EKG. The test was scheduled for the day after Thanksgiving so we would not have to miss time from work. This was the day our lives changed forever...

Off we go to take this routine stress test that we never thought anymore about. After all this was the weekend my sister was having her annual "after Thanksgiving party" and we were looking forward to going as we did every year. We would do this and then go back home to get ready for the party.

He was called back for his test while I waited in the waiting room. Time started to pass and I was concerned because he was still back there. I had mixed emotions coming in, because I knew something was wrong, but couldn't understand why I felt this way.

I inquired at the desk, frantic and agitated, as to why he was still back there! Of course they gave me the routine answer, he's not done...no really, I didn't know that! I remember going into the hall to call my daughter and I told her something was not right. Soon after, they came and told me he had been admitted, his lungs and heart didn't look good. Benny was previously diagnosed with sarcoidosis, a condition he had before we met, but his condition was in remission. Now they were thinking it had come back and wanted to run some tests.

Benny and I were married just a few days shy of 25 years, when he went home to be with the Lord. Our marriage was always good...no it wasn't. Why am I lying? But what I wouldn't give to have those bad times back and more. As we all know tomorrow is not promised, so ladies I want you to love, respect, and honor your man.

I remember our wedding day; it was a day I thought would never happen for me. It was something I always dreamed about, as all women do. Finally, I was getting married to the man I lived with for 8 years. Did I love him, yes, but I felt I deserved to get married. After all, we lived together all that time, had fun doing drugs and the sex was great. Isn't that why *everyone* gets married?

Umm, NO, as I later found out. I felt I got married for all the wrong reasons, and then I disliked being married. We fought a larger part of the time; he mentally abused me and made me think less of myself. He was jealous of my daughter, who was 12 years old, and she didn't like him. I felt like a rag doll being pulled, afraid my arms would be ripped out of its socket for giving in to the other. Ok, he's happy, but now she is complaining, she's happy and he is mad and not talking to anyone. This went on for years! I was saved, sanctified, filled with the Holy Ghost (so I was told) and desired to leave my husband. No one from the church was trying to stop me, minister to me, heck, some even encouraged me.

I was attending church every Wednesday and Sunday, praising God and disliking my husband. What's wrong with this picture? So I made an appointment to speak with my Pastor regarding our marriage. I told him what was going on and he said I could separate, but could not get a divorce. Not what I wanted to hear! You are kidding me, right? I continued to live with my husband; we lived like room-mates, we were unhappy and miserable. I thought after all, God is going to work this thing out.

I needed more in my life and I decided it was time for a change. My marriage was still in shambles and the God at *this* church wasn't doing anything. I left the Baptist church to attend a non-denominational church. I *truly* discovered the Holy Spirit, again, so I thought! I couldn't live with this man, we were unequally yoked and he was going to hell! Hey, I was looking for any excuse to justify why I wanted to leave. My daughter disliked him and so did I! So we packed our things and moved out!

Things were going well at my new apartment, but I still remembered what my previous Pastor said about getting a divorce. We lived about 5 minutes from one another; after all, I had to keep a check on him and my house.

During our separation I became ill and he came to the hospital to see me. He would take care of things at my apartment and check my car. We began to talk and then started dating, trying to work things out. He told me he would change and make everything right if I came home. I said, let's continue to date and see what happens. Well, he did change and I felt it was okay to come back home. My daughter stayed at the apartment and lived her life, it was 1997 when I went back home.

I realized I had to let him see the Christ in me. I began talking to him like he was saved. You know all the clichés we say as Christians, "You don't have to receive that", "blessed and highly favored", "the devil is a liar"; you know what I am talking about ladies. He would just look at me, but it was getting in; spiritual osmosis was taking place. The word says in 1Peter 3 – *Wives, respect and obey your husbands in the same way. Then the husbands who do not obey the word of God will want to know God. They will want to know God because their wives live good lives, even though they say nothing about God.*

He was accustomed to us getting high together every day and selling drugs, now I stopped everything cold turkey! He couldn't believe it! I would hear him tell his friends how I changed. "Man, she doesn't even get high anymore and wants nothing to do with the life." He never knew I heard him and I continued to talk to him like he was saved.

November 24, 2000 would be a day I will never forget. I went from having a husband who was healthy to beginning a journey with no future, full of pain and heartache.

His mother passed during the onset of his disease and he couldn't even attend her funeral. I know this broke his heart, his mother was his life. He was becoming very angry and bitter about his illness and her death and who else could he be mad at but me. He was hospitalized shortly after her passing for the second time of what was to be too many to count.

My husband continued to get worst, he was so edematous (filled with fluid) he couldn't walk or even wear shoes. The worst part of this was we still had no diagnosis! During this process I was working, going to school for my degree, taking care of him, and his mother (until her passing). I believed God, yet at the same time, I was sick of this life. I had to stop working at my dream job because I had to keep calling out. In my own defense, I called out because I had to be with my husband at every doctor visit. There was something going on, I knew it was serious, and we still had no answers. I was attending a church where I had to beg for help; everyone was saying what they were going to do all the while doing nothing. I remember one time one of the ministers kept telling me he was going to come see Benny and never did. I was getting offended and the Lord told me I had to confront him. Well our conversation resulted in him coming to see Benny that day.

Saints, don't make empty promises to hurting people, it exasperates the issue and can cause offense. Now, you have folks leaving the church for what? I won't even tell anyone I will pray for them if I am not nor have any intention of doing so. Please don't misconstrue my truth, just being very transparent. I think I correlate this to my own situation when I needed prayer, an ear, or help.

I was hurting, my husband was hurting and getting worst and no one was helping me/us. I knew God had it and us, but sometimes, let's just be real, you need the tangible.

Also, understand when you are a healthcare professional, when those bad reports come, you know what they mean. I will not lie, I would hear things that would cause me to forget I was a child of the most high God, as was my husband! I knew this was critical and he could die. I would be like this for the day, but praise God, morning by morning new mercies I see. I would be back on focus knowing who the Great Physician was! I had good and bad days, but always trusting God. I had to be strong for Benny! I would *never* allow him to see me weak or crying.

We decided to get a second opinion in Philadelphia at Jefferson where I was currently working. Everyone assured me, this doctor was going to help him get better! We went to one of the top pulmonologists and I wanted to kill him. He had as much bed side manner as satan has mansions in Heaven which explains his non-empathic character. Yes, I know you have to walk in the persona of a professional, but for one of your colleagues you could at least give them *some* respect. Oh that's right, I had forgotten most doctors think the MD behind their names rightfully represents their GOD status.

I had to push Benny in a wheelchair as his edema grew worst. He took us directly to his office, not stopping to change into a gown or take vitals. Reminded me of monopoly, "go directly to jail, don't pass go and don't collect $200". Something serious was wrong and I had to be strong in front of Benny. My medical background would often get in the way of being a wife at times like this, but God blessed me with this gift so I walked in it.

He delivered a fatal blow, there "is nothing I can do for him, he needs two lungs." We both became stoic to the point of not even being able to move! I tried to remain composed, but asked if there was a ladies room. I immediately left the room and began hysterically crying. Oh my God, what does this mean, I knew what it meant, but I was grasping for straws. I had to compose myself and go back in and act accordingly. We left the office and the return trip home seemed like it took years. I was quietly sobbing behind him as I pushed his wheelchair; I knew he couldn't see or hear me. As I approached the valet, I got myself together and proceeded with the ride home.

As I was driving my emotions took over and I began crying and sobbing to the point I had to pull over. I never cried in front of him another day during the 14 years of his illness. I will never forget the words my husband spoke to me on that day... He said, "Valerie, you know how you're always talk about God and trusting Him, well, we have to trust Him for this." I had no words except, You are right." Don't tell me you can't have what you speak! Ladies start/continue to speak life over you husband not matter what it looks like. The enemy will have you to believe it is for naught, but let me tell you, it isn't.

Well, do you think the enemy is going to allow all of that "trust" to take place? When we get home, my husband passed out, couldn't breathe, and was rushed to the emergency room. He was admitted and remained in the hospital for almost two months. Every day I would bring him books on healing, talked to him about healing, and had the TV on the Christian channel.

Mind you, he is still not saved. I would pray and pray and pray. He began to become very, very bitter and angry. He was very sick, not only were his extremities edematous, but his abdomen filled with fluid as well. He was not getting any better.

One day a Deacon from my church came to visit Benny and asked him if he wanted to receive Christ as his personal Savior and without hesitation, Benny said yes! I began to cry, because if you remember, I said he was one of the ones definitely going to hell. Wives, if you think God has not heard your prayer for your unsaved spouse, think again! I prayed for Benny, as well as did others, for almost 12 years. Let me tell you, this was the beginning of a metamorphosis like you would never believe.

I remember asking Pastor John, my current Pastor, if my medical background was hindering my husband's healing. I would become alarmed when they would give him bad reports, yet I would know who was in charge. The medical side of me also knew the devastation of his illness. Usually, by the morning I was reconnected to the vine and knew who was in control. I remember Pastor John telling me God made me for Benny and my medical knowledge was just putting the natural on His super.

As the years progressed so did his disease and I was slowly losing my husband as I knew him. Once he was properly diagnosed, he was good for about 10 years. The doctors gave him a short time to live, but God, prayer, and his faith; he had the tenacity of a pit bull and lived for 14 years. He could not work; he was very bitter, angry, and mad at everyone in the beginning. I continued to work and love on him. I knew how unhappy he was, but I was going to do everything I knew to do to make it better. I remember asking God to take any healing he had for me and give it to him. The dislike I had for my husband in the previous years. I can remember being so angry at myself

269

for leaving him and losing that year we could have been together.

Ladies, don't allow the enemy to come to rob, kill, and destroy your marriage. He hates the unity of family and wants to cause division and strife any way he can. We serve a Greater One and you have to believe in your marriage, and pray, and go to war for it. Marriage is work, but it's one job I loved and if I could have my husband back in the same condition, I would welcome him with open arms.

God is bigger than any problem you may have! Speak to every situation, confess the Word over your marriage, family, and children. Step away from the nay-sayers who have nothing good to say about you or your marriage. You know the ones who say "girl if I were you I would..." Believe me, I had a lot of those and I did a good job all by myself. I am somewhat of a loner and the enemy loves loners, he has a front seat in your mind.

In the last five- seven years of our marriage during his illness, there was no more intimacy. I never thought my husband would be saved, let alone become the awesome man of God he became. I was truly blessed and proud to be his wife.

Through all of this, the good/bad times, in sickness and in health, until death do us part, I want to know what you would do in this circumstance? What would you do with a terminal diagnosis? Would you stray because he couldn't fulfill your needs or be the dutiful faithful wife God called you to be? Do you understand the true meaning of the promises you pledged at the altar. This oath is more than just a ceremonial exchange of words. It is a sacred permanent oath, and it serves as the foundation of your marriage. We should refer to the oath as an unbreakable covenant with God first, then our husbands. The Old and New Testaments of the Bible are filled with several references for covenant vows of marriage. My question to you is, what have you done with those words? Did you just say them as part of the ceremony or are you living them daily and what do they mean to you? Are you prepared to honor these vows in sickness and in health unto death? When you make a vow it is important to know that the Bible has strong words for making vows casually. (Matt. 5:33, Exodus 20:7, Num. 30:1-4)

There were times through this 14 year journey I wanted to find someone to share my time with, go out and have fun together, even thought about having an affair. BUT, the one thing I would always think about, my husband may not know, but God knows. He sees everything I do and I would be dishonoring Him as well. I came so close to sleeping with someone on my job. The enemy kept him coming, saying all the right things, giving me all the attention I was not getting at home. I can remember to this day, how my friends continuously would chime in, you should, and after all, Benny is sick and he trusts you, he won't know. OMG, I came so close. Needless to say, the Holy Spirit reminded me of who I was and to whom I belonged and I couldn't do it. I called the aggressor, yes I said aggressor, after all remember who sent him. I told him I could not do this. He was surprised, but I was relieved!

My husband had done so much for me and my daughter. If it were not for him, I would not be the woman I am today. Yes, I would love to make love to him again, go out and do the things we used to do, just spontaneously get up and go, but it was not going to happen. Our last 5 - 7 years together had no intimate moments, yet our love grew and blossomed into an indescribable love, one I will cherish for a lifetime. One I could never have imagined could be so beautiful and romantic. I didn't need the physical penetration to solidify our love, just holding him, kissing him and yes waking up and seeing him breathing was enough. This is in sickness and in health to death do us part. Are you prepared? This is not a contract that can be broken; a covenant is a permanent commitment. It symbolizes the covenant God made with His chosen people. For me, it's my covenant that I made with my husband.

Sickness can come in many facets...heart attack, depression, prostate cancer, and stroke, just to name a few. It will affect each person differently, but you have to be prepared, strong, and ready to fight the enemy for your man. Can you continue to love (faithfully) in sickness and in health, what will you do in an unto death circumstance?

I loved my husband unto life and as I stated previously asked God to give him any healing He had for me. I cannot explain in words my love for my husband. I ask every day for God to give him back. I would take him back in the same situation and take care of him all over again.

I walked this journey in sickness and in health, unto death did we part. My journey these last 14 years had much pain, but purpose was the plan. I would never have believed how many people watched us and still to this day say they want a marriage like ours; if they only knew the story behind the glory. They tell me how Benny impacted their lives and say, teach me how to be a good wife like you. When I look back over the years, I would never have imagined he/us would impact so many. He left me with a new appreciation for faith, perseverance, tenacity, love, and being the best I can. I miss him with every fiber of my being, but I know he is happy now.

Are you ready to live in the excellence of love regardless, can you live beyond the vows? (1Corn13:4-13)

Baby this is for you, *"it is what it is"*... *(Benny's* favorite saying) You were my everything, my forever love; I miss you more each day. THANK YOU for your perseverance on July 10,

8 days before you went home to be with the Lord, to buy my 25-year anniversary ring. Thank you for loving me, it was my honor to love you...see you at the top.

I invite you to look into our lives and walk alongside as you experience our fight with Pulmonary Hypertension and how our love prevailed in the struggle. Look for my book *"Who Ordered These Shoes"* in 2016

Valerie Stancill is the founder of *What Are U Eating? LLC*, a holistic wellness business committed to helping people feel better and live longer by making healthy lifestyle choices. Valerie has recently added patient advocacy coaching to *What Are U Eating? LLC*. She passionately works to help families navigate the complexities of the modern health care system to ensure that medical and health needs are met. She is a certified holistic wellness coach, author, and a manager with NeoLife (GNLD) natural plant-based supplements. Her passion is to educate and equip people to regain control and live abundantly by changing their lifestyles.

Valerie's educational background includes a BS in Health Arts from the University of St. Francis and she became certified as a holistic wellness coach through the Institute of Integrative Nutrition.

A Final Word from Dr. Tina Scott

Standing Through the Storm of Adversity
Dr. Tina Scott

I am sure that after reading the writings of these authors, you may have experienced various emotions. Each one has revealed a personal story and journey with you. If you know any of these authors, you probably view them a little differently now. They stripped themselves and gave you their heart in fragmented pieces and allowed you to experience their journey of pain and healing. A common theme of every story in this book is that every person met a storm of adversity in their marriage, but chose to go through that storm rather than have the storm go through them. Each author, through their adversity, showed resilience by being able to bounce back from a difficult experience. Each displayed behaviors, thoughts, and actions that allowed them to move forward and rebuild after the adversity hit their relationship with their spouse.

I'm curious...have you ever had to go through a storm in your marriage? A storm of anger, a storm of rejection, a storm of unforgiveness, a storm of jealously, a storm of bitterness, grief, sorrow, sadness, loneliness, or pain? Storms like these can be devastating and can wipe you out. They can make you just want to give up and not move forward.

However, as many of the authors have discussed, storms don't have to destroy us. We were made in such a way that we can go through most storms. I say most storms because there are some storms that you should go through and there are some storms that you should avoid. On Aug 29, 2005, Hurricane Katrina hit Louisiana. It was a Category 5 hurricane and everyone was urged to evacuate. Some chose not to leave, and the results were devastating. Many died because this is the type of storm that you should avoid and run from.

Domestic abuse is a Category 5 storm, and this is the kind of storm that should be avoided. If your storm is not a storm of this type, you should follow the examples of these women and go through the storm of adversity, making it through to fight for the kind of marriage that God wants for you.

One of the things about adversity is that it does not discriminate, which means that it is something everyone goes through during this journey called life. We all have experienced trouble, difficulty, hardships, suffering, affliction, sorrow, and misery. If we are not careful, these things can hold us back, slow us down, or make us feel that there is no way out, hindering us from reaching the purpose that God has for us. However, just like the authors in this book, we have to make sure we have tools to cope when adversity comes our way. Even though our journey is different when traumatic and stressful events happen, I have found and used a few tools that have helped me and many others to get through when adversity hits: Pray, acknowledge, keep moving, and get help.

Pray

The first tool that God gives us is the tool of prayer. God wants us to talk to Him, so instead of worrying, pray. Prayer is the way that we communicate with God. Tell God what you are going through and make your requests known because He has the answers. "Be anxious for nothing, but in everything by prayer and supplication, with thanksgiving, let your requests be made known to God. And the peace of God, which surpasses all comprehension, shall guard your hearts and your minds in Christ Jesus." (Philippians 4:6-8)

Acknowledge

Acknowledge what you are going through. Every marriage

goes through some measure of adversity. Take off the mask and make a connection with your pain without blowing it out of proportion. We often try to hide our pain from others as well as from ourselves. We think that if we ignore the reality of our pain, it will vanish. I am sure you understand that this is a grave fallacy.

Experience should have taught you that the more you ignore something, the more the problem will manifest itself into a bigger monster which will only work against you. We try to ignore the monster by displaying outward signs that we are happy. We smile, joke, and talk just to avoid the inner turmoil that we are feeling. When you do this, you feel a deep void and an unremitting emptiness. You start sensing inner turmoil. The inner turmoil spreads like a cancer. It goes straight to the heart, and then attacks the mind. This keeps you up at night and has you rising early in the morning. It is depriving you of inner peace and joy that is possible, not only in your life as an individual, but in your marriage as well.

I have found from my personal and professional experience that one must be willing to accept the fact that they are going through something, meaning that they must acknowledge that the unwelcomed guest of adversity has come knocking at the door. And even though you may not want to answer, adversity will often kick your door in and invade your space. When your space has been invaded by such an unwanted guest, don't retreat. Do not give up. It may be hard and it may be challenging to press through, especially when everything and everyone seems to be encouraging you to quit, but you have to stand. Stand on the Word of God and know that He is standing right with you.

In your marriage, maybe you can relate to a few of the scenarios below:

- The wife who is working hard to make her marriage better, but has a husband who won't even talk about it or try.
- The husband who works over-time to address the financial imbalance in the home while dealing with a resentful, neglected wife.
- Being one of the hardest workers on the job, only to be passed over for a promotion.
- Going to bed every night with your mate, feeling like you are climbing into a coffin.

Ask yourself why you are feeling the way that you do over this situation. Own what you need to own as it relates to the situation whether it is good or bad. Identify what is triggering you. Stand, acknowledge, and implement strategies to move forward together.

Keep Moving

One of the main suggestions I give my clients is to keep moving when adversity hits. I encourage them to look for opportunities in their movement to find some self-discovery. Believe it or not, we can learn from our struggles and develop a greater sense of strength. Never allow yourself to be a victim to your own thoughts. Instead, nurture a positive view of yourself and your situation. In doing this, you will develop the confidence to move forward. The key is to keep moving.

I remember hearing a story that a preacher told during one of his sermons. There was a man that asked his daughter to drive because he was tired. The daughter agreed to drive, and as she started driving, it began to rain. The rain got heavier and heavier and the daughter asked her father whether she should pull over and stop. The father told her to keep driving. But it started raining harder. Nervous and scared, the daughter questioned her father again, and again, her father told her to keep moving and not to pull over.

Nervous and scared, she continued to drive until eventually, she has made it out of the storm to where it was sunny once again. At that point, the father told the daughter to pull over and to look in the rearview mirror. When she looked back, she could see the storm was still going on behind her and the cars that had pulled over were still in the storm. I tell this story to encourage you to keep moving when you are going through, because if you remain still, you will remain in your place of pain and adversity that will keep beating you and weighing you down. If you keep moving, you will be able to get through and put the storm behind you.

Get Help

Get help when adversity hits. You should seek help from your pastor or from a professional therapist. It is okay to seek help for yourself, as well as for your marriage. The best marriage suffers from wear and tear over the days and years. If you notice that you and your partner are growing apart, not speaking, having a lack of intimacy and other signs that you are breaking down, professional marriage counseling should be your next step. I know that you don't want anyone in your business. How can someone on the outside help? Let me ask you something…is what you currently doing working? If the answer is no, then put your pride aside and save your marriage. Allow someone that is trained to help you get back on track. Allow therapy to be your laboratory to explore, experiment, and practice dealing with thoughts and behaviors that have been breaking you down and breaking down your marriage. Your marriage is worth it and so are you. Feel free to contact me directly for help by visiting my website at DrTinaScottLPC.com.

Dr. Tina Scott is a wife and a mother of three children. She is a psychotherapist and runs a private practice where she specializes in bereavement and relationship recovery. Dr. Tina also has a contract with the Wounded Warriors program, where she offers clinical support to soldiers suffering from Post-Traumatic Stress Disorder. A well sought after public speaker, Dr. Tina lends her expert insight on Old School 100.3 FM in a radio spot called, "Moments with Dr. Tina" as well as on the viral Internet radio show, "Diva Docs." On the 3rd Sunday of each month she is a guest on the show, Physicians on Air, on WURD 900 AM. In the community, Dr. Tina serves on the boards of WIC and Habitat for Humanity. In the church she is a dedicated leader on the Marriage Enrichment Ministry. Dr. Tina's life scripture is Jeremiah 29:11, "For I know the plans I have for you," declares the LORD, "plans to prosper you and not to harm you, plans to give you hope and a future.."

Thank you for reading *Wives on Fire!* It is our prayer that something was said to enrich your life and strengthen your marriage. We give God ALL THE GLORY for great things He has done!

It is not by accident that you are holding this resource in your hands. We pray that it becomes a tool and a reference to aid you in navigating this precious journey of life and marriage. If you would like to learn more about TrulyWed Wives, please visit our website, www.TrulyWedWives.com, or visit our Facebook page.

You are not alone! God is always with you and He will see you through. God has provided this support system of wives who are here to help you. Know that we are praying for every person who reads this book and their marriage. We are committed to the support of Christian marriages worldwide.

Thank you for supporting this ministry. We are looking forward to even greater things in the future! God Bless!